In My Own Words
(Still Running)

In My Own Words (Still Running)

Mickey Finn

authorHOUSE®

AuthorHouse™
1663 Liberty Drive
Bloomington, IN 47403
www.authorhouse.com
Phone: 1-800-839-8640

First published by AuthorHouse   05/16/2011

ISBN: 978-1-4567-7999-3 (sc)
ISBN: 978-1-4567-8000-5 (ebk)

Printed in the United States of America

Dedicated to my Mom and Dad
who gave me life.

Foreword

As an Irish national it gives me no pleasure to assist in recording an account of the heartbreaking tribulation of those boys who, largely through no fault of their own, were sent to St Joseph's Industrial School in Letterfrack, County Galway. The road to hell being paved with good intentions this monstrous and now notorious penal colony; let's call a spade a spade, for children began life and for some, death, as a Quaker-inspired school in 1887.

Through the passage of time it transformed into what was euphemistically called an industrial school (*Scoileanna Saothair*) for young boys. Today they are called Children's Detention Schools. Under the Industrial Schools Act (1888) their purpose was to 'care for neglected, orphaned and abandoned children.' In essence they were a dumping ground for children who found themselves on the fringes of society. In 1954 there were three classes of boys placed in Letterfrack's St Josephs: The Homeless and those guilty of criminal offences, the destitute sent by local authorities in accordance with the Public Assistance Act; those voluntarily admitted by parents and guardians. From its conception St Joseph's Industrial School was mismanaged by the Congregation of Christian Brothers.

In respect of those committed for criminal acts it should be remembered these unfortunates were extremely young and their 'offences' petty in the extreme.

It is a sobering thought that within our lifetime conditions at this school find their equal only in 18th Century English judicial barbarism. The nearby Fields of Athenry are poignant enough for most people's stomachs.

For many of the unfortunate boys who endured St Joseph's transportation might well have been a blessing.

The 'school's' notoriety was founded upon the abuse and extreme physical and mental punishments inflicted upon defenseless children by a largely psychotic mob of cassocked ecclesiastic wardens. No fewer than 147 children died whilst under their tender mercies. Many of these brothers may be presumed to be practitioners of the dark arts. Only the devil could have been inspired to inflict such miseries on defenseless waifs; only darkness have conspired a whole community to turn aside from the wailing of hundreds of children through those dark decades of its existence. Some of the dreadful scenes are reminiscent of the scenes depicted in medieval tapestries in which the excesses of hell are defined.

In My Own Words Still Running is the testimony of Mickey Finn, himself an inmate from the age of eleven to sixteen. It is also an authentication, a memorial and recognition for each of the adolescent victims of those men of the cloth and their collaborationists. His account of life in this dreadful institution will give many pauses for thought as to the iniquities of man. It immortalizes the cold ethos of the judiciary. They will also be inspired by the selfless acts, rebelliousness and inborn stoicism of young boys in the face of extreme hostility.

Mickey Finn.

Chapter 1

"Jesus!" I thought to myself as I awoke during the dark hours of the early morning; "What is that sticky stuff on my leg?"

The smell in the airless room was fetid; hardly surprising as it was home to an entire family. I was in bed between my two brothers; still fast asleep the both of them and I could feel something on my leg which my mind interpreted as skutry shite. Has someone shit the bed I mutter to myself in the darkness?

Like a foul-smelling blanket the oppressive night air desensitized my senses. Drifting off again was the preferred option given the only other thing I could do was check the unwanted sensation out. I am so tired; 'fuck it,' I thought: 'I will see what it is in the morning. As I drift between wakefulness and slumber I can hear someone moving about in the darkened room. Someone is going to use the piss bucket. Pssssssssssssssssssssss, you could clearly hear the stream gushing out of my da's bladder. His dropping the bucket's lid did nothing to remove the stench of urine and body odor. I am struggling to get back to sleep but eventually I drift off.

Our family lives in a one-room terraced tenement situated in North Great Georges Street in Ireland's capital city, Dublin. It is a four storey building with the ubiquitous basement somehow holding it all up. There's five of us; children that is; then there is me ma and da. Where we are living or rather existing now is probably the sixth place we have lived in since I was ushered into the world and I am not yet eleven years old.

This place is what you get when you have been evicted from your home by Dublin Corporation, the great Irish housing authority who is a law unto its self and is controlled by lowly civil servants, who do not seem to answer to any authority outside of their own little circle.

This is rejects Ville with all its attendant baggage of poverty; the bowed and the broken; the debris of Ireland's lower classes.

The foul and cramped tenement is owned by one of the largest estate owners in the Irish Republic; the religious orders of God. Could there by anyone on earth so religious as to consider their charity so generous; charging rents for a single room accommodating no less than seven impoverished family members? A manger in a stable would be a major step upwards; anything but this. Here they expect the grateful pious residents to live not in squalor but in harmony. Yes, for them it is our privilege to be able to get to our feet when the first bars of the Irish national anthem are played following the 11.30am mass. Suffer the little children, from those pious brethren who afterwards retreat to their overburdened tables in the opulent mansions of ecclesiastical benevolence. Wouldn't your heart go out to the piety?

Our room is 16ft by 12ft; wall to wall just four strides apart; the room's bleak landscape is broken only by two burlap flour sacks keeping the light and the cold winter air on the outside. If you do pull the sacking aside and peer out you will gaze out over a tiny backyard set against a factory wall. In the room itself there are three beds, two chairs, a small table, and a sink unit with a couple of presses atop it.

My two brothers and I share a single bed. One of them is much older and has recently returned from an industrial school; a euphemism for a house of correction for juvenile offenders. I have just a vague recollection of seeing him on earlier occasions; I think when I was about six-years old. There was little bonding between us. I hardly understood the brogue he had adopted, which hadn't improved since his return.

He I was led to believe was taken from his mother at birth by the heavenly Nuns, and placed into various institutions' for the first sixteen years of his life. My other brother is about five-years old.

Our two sisters share their own single bed; they're ten and seven-years old whilst ma and da have the comfort of the remaining double bed. When we kick our bare feet out in the mornings we are reminded of the coldness of the torn linoleum partly covering the bare floorboards. The wallpaper, no doubt resplendent when long ago it was applied, is stained with damp and in parts is already showing the effects of gravitational pull. Hanging precariously from the grey ceiling is a single un-shaded light bulb. The bucket-loo can be dispensed with during the day as there is a small communal toilet in the backyard used by those privileged to live in such salubrious accommodation; the commode is far too good for a priestly backside.

Our home was at least central to Dublin's bars and perhaps as a reminder of our saintly heritage just a short walk away from the internationally famous O'Connell Street and the other Irish 'saint'; Parnell (Street). Both should be spinning in their graves having had their names attached to such human wretchedness and vice.

I am awake now or at least conscious of the clattering of the teapot that tells me ma is preparing the morning ritual pot of tea. My spirits lift for the sticky stuff I had felt on my bare leg was it seems a figment of my sleep-filled imagination; nor is there a stain to be seen.

"Ma, I felt some sticky stuff on my leg in the night: It woke me up as well as did da when he was pissing in the bucket."

Mother was wearing a worn and stained dressing gown and even though her blond hair was yet to be brushed and combed she looked ethereally beautiful to me.

Ma looked at me with those bright green eyes of hers: "Sure, it was only a bad dream you were having. We all get them from time to time."

I wasn't entirely persuaded and I am not sure she was convinced by her own reassurances either. Her unease was noticeable and I could almost read her mind: "Oh, God. I hope it isn't what I think it is; the oldest of my sons' playing with himself despite his sharing the bed with his two younger brothers. What's to be done; I haven't a spare bed for him."

There weren't many options for the hard-pressed mother. With five children to feed and clothe and on my da's meager wages too there was little enough left to feed the insatiable appetite of my father's drinking and gambling habits. She herself was third or fourth down the pecking order whilst the moneylender could go and whistle when we heard him knock on the door we would all be quite in the hope he would go away. My da seemed able to find him when he wanted money, but was never here when he would call to be repaid. Such women managed.

Da' was up and about now and the sink, which he routinely washed and shaved himself in, seemed far too small for his large frame as he bent over it. There was the alternative larger bowl in the yard outside he sometimes used for a proper wash. The emptying of the night bucket was below his dignity though; this chore was left to me or my sister's. His having helped to fill the pot seemed to have no bearing in the matter; in some ways the socialist philosophy of all for one and one for all was lost on him, when he chose, and this was often.

So off we trot, my sister and I, each holding our own side of the bucket's wire handle. It occurred to me as we stepped out into the dark hallway leading to the steps descending to the yard that this morning it seemed heavier than usual.

All was going perfectly well until I slipped on something, perhaps a puddle of piss or some other piece of rubbish, that would often litter the stairway. Unable to catch myself my sister screamed a warning but losing my balance I was horrified to see the bucket and its contents tumbling and spilling down the staircase. Above the din of the falling bucket cascading its contents down the stairway my sister's shrill warnings that da will kill the both of us.

My attempts at hurriedly cleaning up the mess were futile; I had neither the means nor the will on account of how great the mess was. Nor did I have the time for I could already hear the threatening tread of da coming down the stairs in response to the noise. Wham! I felt the thud of a damp cloth strike the nape of my neck, almost knocking me off my feet. The brief pause only heralded the follow up slap, this time across my face:

"Are you mad or what?" Bawling with his eyes popping with annoyance he demanded to know which of us had spilled the bucket. "Out of my way, you useless pair of gob-shites," he exclaimed: "I will sort this out.

His uttered oaths brought some relief as surely he didn't have time to clean the mess up, kill me, and go to work? We pair ran as fast as our legs could carry us towards the back yard's washing and toilet area. Even there the smell of urine was persistent; fresh air is at a premium in these tenements.

There is a sit down toilet but the seat disappeared to God knows where a long time ago. Beside it is a small enamel sink set against the wall. The concrete floor is bare of any comforting linoleum or rug. The toilet door no longer locks and there being no light at all there is plenty of evidence that previous visitor's aims are a little hit and miss. Occasionally, ma puts bleach into our night bucket and splashes it everywhere around the toilet she does her best to make it clean but the stench persists.

As my sister and I are using the facility da roughly barges in on us both: "Are you two finished yet; I have my work to go to. Move over, you daft pair."

Our da drives a coal lorry so no amount of washing is going to scour his skin clean; the use of cold water can hardly help for the soap hardly suds up at all. Happily there's no discrimination against the hard working poor in the pub he frequents and is the one place where he is at peace with himself. His truck is a tipper that carries its spare wheel under its rear axle. When he tips the deck the coal slithers down to fill up the hub of that spare wheel, the contents of which he sells too. For this bonus he has ready customers and it is what he calls his little nixer.

With the morning's mishap behind us I call goodbye as I set my feet towards Marlborough Street School, just a five minute schoolboy's amble away. My mood is carefree for today's lessons will be taken by Mr. Cleaney. He has a pleasant and patient temperament and hasn't any favorites. He treats the kids from the poorer backgrounds with patience and understanding. The school itself is imposing; a rather grand stone brick affair that is home to the Irish Language School too. I am fond of my school where my own class of about 40 pupils is situated on the first floor. It is a light airy room with three vast windows and an impossibly high ceiling.

It must have been about eleven o'clock one morning; all is studiously calm when the silence is broken by a gunshot from the back of the classroom. Jesus! There's a mad scattering, kids ducking and weaving in every direction. Surely there's a mad gunman in the school? I think as I dive under my desk out of the way.

Mr. Cleaney was the model of calmness and I have no doubt his kind calmly sang hymns from the stern of the Titanic when it sank below the waves.

A youngster sitting at the rear of the classroom, having found a live bullet had brought it to school with him. With a schoolboy's natural curiosity he had been probing the bullet with a heated pin when it detonated. The result was that two of his fingers ended up somewhere distant in the classroom. Needless to say there was little work done for the rest of that day.

There were times when the school would give us 'poor boxes' so that we might make collections on the school's behalf. My own contribution was to learn adeptness at opening them with a butter knife; for weren't we poor too? We also targeted a nearby bakery in order to help make ends meet. It wasn't beyond our wit to liberate a few loaves of bread for me ma's empty table. Batch loaf being me da's favorite. Those whose courage failed to desert them could venture even further into the bakery to lay their thieving little hands on the cakes that were baked there.

The sharpest tool in the box was a boy named Redser. He was a dab hand at locating where the bigger chocolate gateaux were shelved; in fact he was so good at it that we became sick of chocolate cakes. Emboldened by his growing reputation as a sneak thief he moved onwards and upwards. One day he slipped into the egg carrier's van and made off with a small bag of the man's takings. Redser later appeared, flaunting £20, £10 and £5 notes; booty from which I was given a total of £60.

Unfamiliar with such wealth I hid and kept the notes for two weeks. I wasn't quite able to perceive their value but the egg carrier surely had and the heat was on. The word had got around and local shopkeepers were keeping their eyes open for youngsters using notes to make purchases. When I finally decided to spend the money it was to a local shop called The Mullingar: The owners I think they were from Cork County.

My purchasing a pennyworth of sweets with a £20 pound note aroused immediate suspicions and in no time at all the Garda was upon me. This was to be my first encounter with the stalwart culchie; the police force known in Ireland as The Garda. With little choice in the matter, for I was handcuffed to a police officer, I was ushered into the patrol car with another of the officer's holding me by the scruff of the neck. He had noticed the handcuffs were far too large for me and feared I might take to my feet. In no time at all I was being pushed through the doors of Store Street Garda Station. Terrified by my surroundings and the manner of the police officers I confess to wetting my pants.

Taking me through to an ante room there was much to remind me of the gravity of the situation; the room was bare except for a table and two chairs, both the table and its two chairs were screwed to the floor. I was motioned to sit on one; an officer towered above me. I think had I stood up my head might just have reached his belt buckle: "Where did you get all that money from, you fucking little bastard?" "And don't lie to me." He growled.

By this time the tears were flowing freely and I was screaming for my ma. "You'll get your ma alright. "You'll get your ma alright," he swore: "Now tell me, lad. Where did you get that fucking money?" I felt a blow to the back of my head that nearly knocked me from the chair.

"Speak up; where did you get that fucking money from," he kept repeating over and over again, hitting me until I began to lose track of time or even see an ending to the torment. My head was swimming with fear and confusion: I had no idea how to respond. Eventually paperwork was brought in and I was charged with theft. From what or who they never did say; it seemed my being unable to account for the money was my only crime.

Leaning over close enough for me to feel his hot breath he told me there had been a spate of burglaries from gas meters. Why not admit to some of them, he said: "Admit it, son, and the judge will go more leniently on you."

I was an eleven-year old skinny runt of a lad; hardly the Al Capone of Dublin but the policemen didn't seem to notice the difference. Maybe it takes a special kind of person to be a copper; they tarred everyone as a criminal regardless of age or circumstance. They seemed to have no sense of proportion. I often wonder how many juveniles they turn to criminality through their over zealousness and brutality. I had the occasional cuff off my da but never a beating as such. My ma was a loving soul no matter what the circumstances. Only time would tell the effects of what these two uniformed pillars of society were to inflict on such a young child. They saw it as just another arrest; the banality of routine. I saw it as my genesis and they provided the baptism of a life, the story of which I will leave the world to decide.

Chapter 2

The inevitable court case loomed and I was to appear in the children's court deep in the heart of Dublin Castle. I am looking my best and am dressed in my Sunday clothes, and my ma is also getting herself ready; as though she is going to church and it is true to say a few prayers were being said. "Son," she says: "I hope this will learn you a lesson and that you will never steal again."

"I never stole anything, ma," I protested. Redser did and he gave it to me. They never got the rest of the money, ma. I hid it under a slate on the roof outhouse, in a little tin box." A tramp I knew had helped me to change it to smaller denominations after he had taken his share of it.

To get to the castle we both walked down O'Connell Street and on to the Quays. From there we crossed the Halfpenny Bridge, up Parliament Street and into the courts. Inside there were many children, most with their mothers and fathers hanging around outside the court house. Some of them were dressed in their Sunday best. It was these parents who knew the score and knew that the better they presented themselves and showed respect to the courts the lighter the sentences would be. The less knowing were badly dressed and I supposed I was somewhere in the middle. All there was left to do was wait until one's name was called. So we just hung around outside the main door, surrounded by young kids smoking fags as if their life depended on it.

I could see the copper who was dealing with my case standing in the background. It was to him I owed this dilemma. There were also other boys I knew; among them I could see Redser, Jobo and Hatchet.

"What are you doing here?" Jobo asked plaintively. I told him I was up for theft but I hadn't thieved from anyone. Redser did know why I was there but he was keeping quiet.

I had never squealed on him, nor had I told anyone where I got the money from. The three of them were in court for an unrelated offence; they had been caught stealing from a large department store in the city centre.

Hearing my name being called I allowed myself to be led into the court by a court clerk who with the passage of time I was to get to know better. Inside the dark panelled court, filled with the curious, court reporters and functionaries sat a woman judge. I was the centre of unwanted attraction as I was instructed to stand facing the judge with my ma standing just a little behind me.

The Clerk of the Court read out the charge made against me: The theft of £20 from a person or persons unknown. The judge held my gaze and her words seemed frozen in the court's silence: "Did you steal this money, young man?"

"No; I got it for my birthday."

"And your birthday; when was it?"

"Last year," says I. There was a sniggering from around the court as my piping voice gave her my explanation.

Exasperated, the judge then enquired as to whether or not I had a mother and father. The policeman standing in the witness box confirmed I had both parents. She asked if the father was known to the policeman, to which he replied he was not. Her next question, again directed to the policeman, was to ask if my father was a working man.

"I believe so, ma'am."

"That being the case I am fining you ten shillings and you have one month to pay: Next case please."

Uncomprehendingly I turned to my ma: "What's happening, ma?" She told me to shush and added that she would explain a little later. As we walked from the court the assembled boys were filled with curiosity.

"What did you get?"

"A fine; I got fined ten shillings." I told them.

"You lucky bastard," says Redser, which was ironic considering that it was his fault I was there at all.

Outside in the fresh air I felt some self confidence returning. As we headed towards home, ma says to me: "I will take you past Hector Greys and get you a little something." Hector Greys is a shop in Liffey Street that is like an Aladdin's Cave full of goodies that all kids love.

It seemed everything was going in the opposite direction to the one I had imagined. The shop is crammed with children's toys. This is the shop to which Uncle William; my godfather had taken me on my 10th birthday. He had invited me to choose anything from the window. I had chosen a cowboy outfit, which fitted me perfectly. I imagined myself to be the perfect likeness of the Lone Ranger. Ma's suggestion that I buy a yo-yo wasn't quite as generous but the unexpectedness more than made up for it.

Having been dealt with by the court I soon learned that as a rite of boyish passage I now had what is called 'form.' This had consequences that would never be welcome; it meant the Gardai could pick me up as and when they pleased; by my misdemeanor I had exposed myself as a potential criminal. They also had the power to visit our home as and when they wished.

They wasted little time in putting their advantage to what they might call good use. Returning home from school a week later I was pounced upon by a Gardai in plain clothes. The reason for his stopping me was my having stuffed my school satchel up my pullover:

"What have you got up there, you little shite?" he barked as he roughly pulled the bag from under my school jumper.

There was disappointment writ large on his face as he searched through the bag only to find school books. Contemptuously spilling them over the pavement he kicked the now empty bag across the pavement.

This was observed by passers-by, one of whom rushed over and confronted him. He could clearly see I was frightened and upset by the encounter: "You fucking idiot, you rozzer," the man said with measured disdain for the police officer. "He's only a child for God's sake: Why don't you pick on someone who's your own size you big thick."

As the policemen snorted and strode on his way I realised I was now a marked kid.

Chapter 3

T hings at home weren't looking too good either. Da had lost his job and was already ranting that there was no way he would be able to pay the ten shilling fine. Ma, at her wits end, said she would try to find the money; she was equally determined I wouldn't be taken away from her. I am confused by the fuss and unclear as to what being taken away meant. More important to me was Redser telling me that as I had not squealed to the rozzers I was welcome to become one of his trusted inner circle.

But I remembered that I still had some of the money hidden in a tin in the back yard, but would it be wise to produce it? To pay the fine? I taught it was better not to mention it.

Redser he now has got a more daring plan that involves taking money from the bakers' vans rather than just bread and cakes. As I am small I am given the task of hanging around the bakery's gates and to act as an observer. No one is going to take much notice of a youngster. Redser told me that I was to note when the firm's drivers returned from their rounds and to note their routine on parking their vehicles. After three days of this I was feeling discouraged; I couldn't see there being any likelihood of their leaving their takings in the vans. Redser doesn't appear too pleased at my disappointment and feeling deflated we left things at that. Already their wayward minds are focusing on other victims.

Redser, Jobo and Hatchet are pupils at a school known as the redbrick slaughterhouse' and it is situated at the top of Summerhill. Each day they go to the school just for an hour during which time their names are registered as being present. Then, during the mid morning break; over the wall they go to spend their day as they wish.

The teachers know well what is going on; perhaps they are equally glad to be rid of their wayward charges, or fear their elder brothers who are adept at intimidation.

I do go to school each day and stick to the routine but I am under pressure from Redser's group to join them in their daily shenanigans. I seem to be getting more involved but being so young I can't figure my way out of their influence. It isn't long before I too am mitching from school with them.

The first occasion I do so I hide my schoolbag in a derelict building in Gardiner Place. As I do so I see a man eying me up and down from a balcony of a block of flats nearby but it doesn't concern me; a schoolbag is hardly likely to be of any interest to him. That day we spent at St Stephen's Green. There wasn't much to do except wander, chat between ourselves and look at the park's ducks. The only excitement was when on our way back we each grabbed an apple from a barrow boy's stall and ran like the wind; a great craic.

The fun ended when returning to the derelict building where I had left my schoolbag I found it had been taken: Fuck! I am in the shite big time, I thought to myself. What do I do now? Ma was getting the dinner ready when I arrived home without my bag and being distracted by her chores she failed to notice: "How was school today?" she calls.

"Great, ma."

"Tell me; what did you learn today?"

"I don't know, ma. I am not sure."

"Typical kids," she says to no one in particular. "Go out and play awhile but don't go too far away. I will call you in when your dinner's ready."

Playing as the last thing on my mind as I sat on the steps with my chin on my knees moodily contemplating my predicament: Fuck; where the hell am I going to get another bag and books? Dejected I forget my mother's advice that I stay close to home. Wandering down Parnell Street to Gardiner Street I hope to see Redser who can perhaps come up with something to get me out of the mess. Again I am in trouble because of my association with my wayward friend.

Turning into Hill Street I bump into skinny Sally who asks me how I am. I tell her that I am grand though I am sure I don't look it. Sally is a bit older than I am; perhaps fourteen but I couldn't be certain. A bit of a hussy with blonde mousey hair she is making the most of her prepubescent curves. The skirt she is wearing reveals what she had for lunch that day but the attention she gets is clearly what motivates the girl.

"Maybe you want to go for a walk then." she says invitingly: "We could just walk up to Mount Joy Square and maybe lie on the grass for a little while?"

Jesus! Lie with Sally on the grass? There is no way I am going to fall for that one; me being not too sure of what she would want to do in the park when we got there. Some of the lads say she is hot, whatever that means. There is no way I am going to find out either as telling her I am on a message for my ma I take to my heels.

My next encounter was much more promising: Redser and Hatchet are standing on the corner of Gardiner Street with cigarettes and looking cool. "You want a drag?" Redser asks as he offers me his cigarette. I don't smoke of course but thinking maybe I should do so I take it from him.

Taking a big drag in imitation of them my head begins to spin; a queer feeling similar to feeling sick comes over me and involuntarily I begin to cough my guts up. My reaction has the boys' in fits of laughing; they can hardly control themselves: They are like those cartoon characters holding their bellies and guffawing.

Wiping the tears from my streaming eyes with my sleeve I wonder how they can smoke these things without reacting the same way. "What's the story anyway," asks Redser after the coughing fit has subsided and I have recovered my wits. It was the opportunity to tell him about my lost bag and books. He agrees that it is a sad outcome to our day's adventures.

Hatchet has an idea: "Maybe you can get to school early in the morning and rob someone's bag, get the books from it dump the bag, and then all you have to do is get a new bag."

It seemed a good idea and would leave just the minor problem of arranging each book's dust cover. My mum had used wallpaper; I wondered if she had any left. I was fast learning the arts of resourcefulness.

"We're going on a job later," adds Redser: "Come with us if you want to. We need someone to keep nix."

"What's happening," I ask.

"Well," he says: "We've got a trolley and we want to get a couple of bags of turf. We can get two bob for them.

The trolley is made from a couple of wooden planks nailed together, with pram wheels or ball bearings attached to make it mobile. We would often take it in turns to ride down Hill Street on such trolleys. I agreed to go with them; it seemed innocent enough.

Going to the depot at the Diamond we can see groups of men stacking sacks of turf. The bags look heavy to me but I hold my tongue. Creeping unnoticed to the side of the shed I take a peek to make sure the coast is clear. It is and whilst I am peering out Redser and Hatchet grab two bags of turf between them. Loading them on to the trolley we run together, pulling the trolley in unison with me desperately trying to stop the two bags of turf from falling off.

"Geronimo!" screams Hatchet having successfully made our getaway as we boys turned into Sean Mac Dermott Street. At No 14 there is a Mr. Knobbly who is something of a Fagan and always prepared to buy what Redser has to offer. Each of my friends received one shilling each whilst I received nothing for my part. "You have to learn more about the job before you are cut in," explains Redser.

All I can think of is that I am a mug. My da is right when he says I am a little gobshite. Telling the two I was off for my dinner I headed back by way of Tuggers; a street famous for its second-hand clothes stalls on a Saturday morning. It isn't an activity one admits too and when going from stall to stall buyers keeps an eye open for anyone who might recognize them so they can disappear unnoticed into the throng.

Our family got a lot of its clothes from the St Vincent de Paul handout centre, which is found at the corner of Mount Joy Square. It was there that I got my communion suit and shoes. "Tuggers Market is for the poor people," ma tells me. It is made clear to us that we never tell anyone we have shopped there; to tell them instead that we have bought our clothes from Guiney's department store.

Dinner this eventful day is spam and mashed potatoes, which I wolf down. Outside I have noticed working men unloading 45 gallon oil drums and can't wait to see what is going on. I find myself recalling my younger days, if there is any such thing for an eleven-year old boy. My thoughts return to when we lived in Railway Terrace in one of granda's homes. I was at a bonfire and one of the barrels on it was well alight and throwing plumes of acrid smoke into the night air. A kid tried getting its lid off and received massive burns to his hands, which were covered in burning tar. I shall never forget his screams as he was rushed to the hospital.

By the time I have my dinner inside me and scamper down the tenement steps to the street below there's no end of children running across the tops of the standing barrels. Each have their lids on and the tar contents are going to be used resurfacing the road. As I crawl among the barrels, which to me appear like a maze, I spot skinny Sally amongst the playing children.

"Sally. Where are you?" I yell.

"I'm here. What do you want?"

"Come over here; I am in the middle." I can hear her feet stepping over the barrel tops as she searches for me. She can't even see me when straddling the two barrels above my hiding place. "Can you see me?" she calls out.

"Sure I can. I can see you have no knickers on and I now know what you had for lunch." I cheekily call out. My insolence doesn't faze Sally at all: ""Do you want me to squeeze down there with you then?"

I am thinking to myself; God, no. I do not want you here with me and my prayers are answered when she adds: "It might be too tight and too dark."

Telling her I will come out and join her at the steps she agrees that is a better idea. I must admit to being a little nervous. She is older than me and has got a bit of a reputation with the boys; but I am now eager to learn fast even if it is a nail-biting ride. Acting what I hope will appear cool I ask her how she is as she joins me on the tenement steps.

"I'm fine," she says: "I hear you're hanging around a lot with Redser. Is that right?"

"Yea. Why not?"

"He has a bit of a reputation you know; he is a bit of a rogue and everyone knows it. He might get you into trouble. You go to Marlborough Street school don't you?"

Nodding my head I listen as she tells me that her brother, Mucker goes there too. "Do you know him?"

I told her I did not but had heard of him but he doesn't attend school all that often so we don't see him much.

"No, that's right. He just can't be bothered going. He would rather collect empty jam jars and bottles and sells them to the rag and bone man. He says that pays, going to school doesn't."

As I listen to her the penny drops and I am thinking what a good idea. Maybe I could do the same?" Where does he sell them?" I ask her.

Sally is perched on the step beside me and looking thoughtful she replies. "Dominic Street I think; he said something about it but I can't quite remember."

Dominic St? This rings a bell and starts to bring back memories. Dominic Street is where I went to school when I was about six years old. It was a time when my ma and da had been doing a lot of fighting and had separated. As a consequence I had been placed in a nearby orphanage; St Joseph's I seem to recall and it wasn't far from the Plaza cinema either it was at the top left hand corner of Parnell Square. I seem to recall it was an imposing Georgian building with a Red door and steps leading up to it.

Her words brought back mixed memories. I remembered clearly the woman who used to bathe me. She was tall with long brown hair; always with a Consulate cigarette in her lips as she scrubbed me clean. Often she would blow the smoke into my face and I have recollections of its sweet perfumery smell.

It was while I was at the orphanage that I attended Dominic Street School where Orphanage uniform was the required wear for us.

These caused problems because it marked us out as posh gits, the results of which were several beatings from local boys. I had no idea at the time my ma was living with her sister, my Auntie Rosie. I did think she was living in Bluebell and was already planning my escape to rejoin her. My younger sister's and brother were also in some type of home or orphanage at this time

It was on a day when arriving back at the orphanage and changing into my day clothes the lady who bathe me came into the room. I found it disconcerting when she started to rub my bare bum for I could see no reason for her to do so; I wasn't sure I liked it either. After she left the room I dressed myself and then fled down the stairs and out of the orphanage's front door; determined to get to my Auntie Rosie's. I had only the vaguest of ideas as to which direction I should take.

Turning left I followed my feet along to Parnell Square and on to Parnell Street, I recall it was a lovely summery day with a great many people about. Taking a right turn I passed Moore Street where all the market traders were selling their fruit and vegetables. As I walked through the din of raised voices, bantering and bartering I kept my head held high, turning occasionally to make sure no one was following me. Breathless, I passed a lane I knew led to Dominic Street School and then walked a little faster. I chose the route through Capel Street where there were many more people and less chance of my being spotted. I was hoping that if by chance I bumped into the Garda they would think I was heading home from school.

Which way now, I thought as I turned right on to The Quays. By this time I was a long way from the orphanage and somehow knew I had to get to the big court buildings without my being noticed. Luckily I didn't seem to be drawing attention to myself.

I was tired and thirsty but knew I had little choice but to stick to my plan to reach Auntie Rosie's home where I would find my ma. Keeping to the Quays I turned left over Kings Bridge. Taking another right I headed past the railway station along St Johns Road heading in the general direction of Inchicore district. It did occur to me to go into my Auntie Peggy's shop but thought better of it. She owned a shop on Inchicore Road. At this stage I had already been walking for close on two hours. I must keep soldiering on was my only thought. I took a left turn into Tyrconnell Road hoping I was going in the right direction.

Somehow my instincts proved right and it was with relief that this six-year old wanderer found himself at Auntie Rosie's front door in Bluebell. My sharp rapping at the door's knocker quickly brought her to the door and wasn't her face a treat when she saw me? Her jaw dropped and she seemed speechless, as if she was seeing an apparition.

"What on earth are you doing here, young man?" she finally asked. Calling her husband I heard him shouting what is it?

"It is Maureen's young lad."

"Come in," she said ushering me inside and as agitated as a flummoxed hen. "Where is your ma, child," she said as she directed me down the hallway and into the small living room. At this point the anxieties and the tiresome journey began to have its effect on me. Mixed with the relief of finding someone who knew and cared for me brought a swelling up of emotion followed by cascades of tears.

"Oh, you poor wee mite," she says as I sob my heart out. "Here, let me put the kettle on; it is a nice cup of sweet tea you will be needing before any explanations. Where on earth have you been coming from now," she asks as she filled the kettle at the tap.

"From the orphanage," I cried, wiping the tears from my face with the sleeves of my jacket. I tried to tell her what was happening, how I felt in between the sobs.

"The orphanage," she says: "What orphanage are you talking about then? Are you out of your mind; are you making this up?"

In between the sobs I tried to tell her what was happening, unclear as to whether I was making any sense or not. "You just settle yourself down, you poor wee mite. I will get you a sandwich and I won't be very long. Here, wipe your face," she added as she passed me a warm wet cloth after holding it beneath the kitchen tap for a moment.

My auntie was hardly out of the door when she appeared again, this time with the sandwich and then another. I was still wolfing it down me when there was a sharp rat-a-tat-tat at the door. The next moment two uniformed Garda police officers were in the room. "There you are, young man. Come along; you have a home to go to."

The tears came flowing again but this time were added to by wailing: "I want my ma, I want my ma. I can't go back there; I want my ma."

"Now kid," said one of the Garda with a note of sympathy in his voice: "You're going to be alright there: They will look after you."

I just want my ma," I wailed as another flood of tears came and the sobbing continued. As the two officers took me towards the police car I managed to free myself and made a dash for it. Running like a little steam engine I flew over the garden fences, falling and stumbling through the shrubs. I am not going back there I was thinking. I was too small and not as fast as I thought I was. Within moments one of the coppers had me by the scruff of my neck.

Lifted under his arm I was carried towards the car with my two small legs pounding the air. As they pushed me into the patrol car my auntie came rushing out to tell me she would be in touch with my ma and would tell her what had happened.

"Okay, lad; there's no use in you crying. You're going back and you will be well looked after. There is nothing for you to be crying about."

"I don't want to go there," I wailed: "The woman who baths me rubs my bum and I am afraid of her."

At hearing this one of the policemen started to laugh: "That's okay, lad; we all need our bums rubbing from time to time."

Crestfallen and bowed I was deposited back at the orphanage to the delight of the long haired Consulate smoking woman, but not for too long; early the following morning ma arrived to take me home it was then I only found out it was at my aunt's in Sheriff Street she was staying and not in Bluebell.

*   *   *

"Wake up, lad. Have you been dreaming," Sally asked with a friendly shove at my shoulder. You've been in another world and I have been yapping away to myself like an ejit. Anyway, I have got to go now. It's getting late and my da says I have to be in by eight o'clock he thinks that all bad things happen after this hour."

"Okay I murmured; I'll see you again then, Sally." By now my thoughts had already turned to thinking how I can find jam jars and bottles: This could be a nice little earner I am thinking to myself. I vow that the following morning I will be up with the lark. I was and the first words out of ma's mouth: "You're up early; what's got into you this morning?"

"I am meeting one of my mates and we are walking to school together," I lied. The truth is I could hardly sleep thinking of my new career in bottle selling.

There's a house I know at the top of the road on the left hand side; it was once used by some kind of drama group, the members of which left empty bottles in the backyard. I made my way there or rather to the disused site next door that was full of debris and collapsed walls and we lads used to play here.

Climbing through the opening in the rusted sheet of tin covering one of the building's windows I already knew my way around. I had played there before. It is a four storey building that has been left to rot and had been vandalised over the years. All the inner stairs have disappeared along with the building's back wall. This means I can get through to the back yard; easily climb a wall and get into the yard of the building used by the drama group.

There I fine crates of empty bottles; I can already see myself rich beyond my dreams as I look around for something suitable to carry my booty in. There in the yard I find an old wicker basket lying under a window sill and it is soon filled with empty bottles. I have about fourteen in all and the weight isn't beyond me as I manhandle my booty back the way I have come. It took me about half an hour to get back to Dominic Street where I find the rag and bone man going about his day's work: "What have you got there, lad?"

"Bottles!"

Peering at my haul he grimaced that he could give me two pence for them. "Jesus, that's great, mister," I say as I hand the bottles over to him. It seems my dreams have been answered; I have a career ahead of me; financial independence beckons. As I head back towards the drama school I feel like I am walking on air; the cock o' the walk. Stopping at The Mullingar shop I ask the shopkeeper for gob stoppers and jelly babies. She wants to know how much I have to spend as she peers at me over her spectacles.

"Tupence worth," I answer her whilst thinking to myself; "You old biddie."

"Here you are," she says kindly: "Are you off school sick?"

"Sick?" I ask!

"Well, shouldn't you be in school?"

Shite I find myself thinking. "No, I have a day off to look after me ma; she is pregnant again and I am going to help her get the baby."

Telling me I am a good boy she asks me if I would like it to be a brother or sister I will be getting.

"I think it is going to be a brother 'cause me ma has got a big head of cabbage that she is eating, and boys come from heads of cabbage." I am so proud to know this and can't understand why she is laughing as I leave the shop. My thoughts are already focused on rising as early as I can the following morning.

On this occasion things didn't move quite as smoothly. I am once again filling my wicker bag when the back door bursts open and a man careers through. "What the fuck are you doing here," he screams. "Get the fuck out of here or I will call the Garda."

Shite: I am over the wall like a scalded cat and with heart in mouth and covered in builder's dust I career straight into my ma who is coming the other way. "Now, what are you up to," she demands to know. "Where's your schoolbag and why are you coming down the street like that; what aren't you in school?"

"I am stuffed now, I think to myself as I try to dodge her grasp. Not quick enough, she grabs me by my arm: "Young man, don't try to get away; you'll only make matters worse for yourself. Where's your schoolbag and why aren't you in school? Answer me."

Bursting into tears at the futility of it all I tell her what I have been up to. Rather than give me the expected clip across the ear she takes me in her arms and hugging me says we had better not let da know what's been going on. "Come on," she says. "We shall get you to school and go and see your master; see what he can do."

Somehow I was reminded of the occasion when a little younger I had desperately wanted to go to the cinema. I couldn't afford to pay so on arrival at the cinema I started to cry and telling them I was lost and my ma was inside they allowed me through into the darkened picture house.

I must have been in there for hours, thoroughly engrossed in whatever the movie was, before I ventured outside again. By this time it was dark, the first time I had ever been out on my own in the dark and it terrified me.

Not surprisingly my mother was out of her mind by the time I got home; a priest was with her and he wanted to take me away, or so I thought. He was there to give me a good telling off, just to put the fear of God in me.

It was just as well my da wasn't home; he was at sea having secured a rating berth on a ship. Such were my recollections as ma got me to school where she had a quiet word with the teacher about acquiring a new set of books. On reaching home I found there was a new schoolbag waiting for me too. The evening was spent putting wallpaper dustcovers on each of them.

"Son," ma said as we folded and pasted the dustcovers: "You need to go to school; it is so important you do so. I know you don't think it very important but everything you learn will be useful to you in later life. I was hardly the only child not to take too much notice of a mother's word of advice.

Chapter 4

Saturday mornings were something we all looked forward to; it was the Saturday matinee at the flicks as the cinema was then called. It was our habit to go to the Electric Cinema in Talbot Street under the railway bridge and join the 'four penny' rush. In 1964. This got you two movies but you had to sit on hard wooden benches from where you could hardly hear yourself thinking with the rest of the kids hollering. The movie must have made an impression because we all emerged as either cowboys or Indians; the movies certainly fired a child's imagination. I had already made my mind up to make my way to America and be a cowboy when I grew up. It is either that or carry on as we are; using the weekends up by playing in half demolished tenement houses.

This activity is perhaps even more dangerous than that of being a cowboy. I once stood on a rusty nail, which merited a trip to the hospital. I had to be checked out for blood poisoning. It was an accident waiting to happen as we couldn't afford shoe repairs and a sole-sized piece of cardboard being inserted into the shoe would usually put matters right, until it rained and then the cardboard was rendered useless.

Childhood urban myth had it that if you cut your hand between the first finger and thumb you could get lock jaw; an ailment that terrified us. It didn't help that, apart from the obvious, no one seemed to know what lock jaw led to or how long it lasted or what it really was.

A welcome break had been the annual summer holiday to Balbriggan, organised by one of the religious groups. A particularly memorable holiday was when during my eighth year I was chucked into the sea by the older boys. Still wearing my clothes I was floundering and terrified but it was great fun to them; especially as I was a non-swimmer.

I was petrified and screaming. Salt was rubbed into the wounds when on reaching the shore and still spluttering I saw the outline of a figure in the window of the nearby building; it was one of the sisters wearing her white robes. From the window she had watched the entire episode and later, calling me over, scolded me for leaping into the sea with my pants and vest on. She made it clear I would be sent straight home if I were to repeat such foolishness. What a silly old bat, I thought to myself. It is past time she had her spectacles replaced surely she had seen that I had been thrown in?

On this present Saturday morning after the movies I decided to take a walk; to see if I could catch up with things by tracking Redser down. I knew where to find them; they were as usual on the corner of Summerhill and Parnell Street.

"What's the story then?"

"We're going on a job," Redser tells me: "You're in on it if you want."

I remembered the earlier escapade when we stole the turf and I was cut out so I was not about to be taken for another ride. I told them I had to get home.

"C'mon you little shite; we'll cut you in this time."

"What's the score then," I asked.

"We're going to the Town and Muck he says with a slight lifting of the lip, as though relishing the opportunity to challenge the status quo once again. The Town and Muck is reference to the Town and Country Club.

Its where all the country boys and girls would go to dance and meet.

The boys stood on one side of the hall and the girls on the other eying each other up before asking each other to dance I was led to believe.

Looking at me carefully he says: "There's a way in; through the back of the maternity hospital. We got in there last week; it's full of crates of lemonade bags of crisps and bars of chocolate it's a gold mine."

Deciding to join them we trotted off down Parnell Street until we reached the social club, which was surrounded by railings far too high for us to climb over but we were able to manage it by climbing on to each others shoulders. There is a back door which has hardboard covering over its glass window that had previously been broken. It seemed to be an open invitation; a marker placed by an earlier rogue, Redser no doubt.

With practiced ease Redser jerked on the hardboard panel and each of us disappeared through the aperture. Inside it is dark and smells strongly of stale smoke. I can feel the stickiness of the carpet under my feet. "This way," whispers Redser: "The drinks are over here."

Soon my eyes began to adjust to the darkness and in the gloom I can now make out the stage and can see the bar on its right towards which Redser is heading. "Fuck! What's this?" He had discovered a steel box and we can see him shaking it and distinctly hear the rattle of coins inside.

"Fuck the lemonade," he says with voice shaking. "There's money in here; let's get the fuck out of here."

Rushing for the door through which we had made our entrance Jobo flies through it. As he disappears through the opening his velocity is hastened with the assistance of a person outside grabbing the collar of his jacket and roughly dragging him out into the daylight.

"Shite, it's the rozzers," cries Hatchet. "We're well and truly fucked now."

Panic stricken we dash back into the bar itself, desperately looking for somewhere to hide or an alternative escape route. There isn't one to be found and after dashing behind the stage I attempt to make myself as small as possible curling up in a ball. I can already hear footsteps approaching and then a man's voice: "Come out, you little bastards. The game's up. Come on out because if we come in and find you we're going to tan your fucking hides off."

"Fuck off!" shouts Hatchet.

"Shhhhh," whispers Redser: "Let me think for a moment will you? There has got to be another way out of here keep quite while I think."

As he speaks he is tugging on a fire exit door bar. Suddenly there is a clattering as the double doors fly inwards and Redser goes flying back to land on his backside I nearly burst out laughing with seeing the state of him; the money box spilling its contents across the floor. As Redser falls three huge rozzers come running into the hall. One scoops up my roguish friend up with one arm and leaning down picks up the money box. Seeing the game is up I emerged from behind the stage, theatrically with my hands up whereupon I too am roughly grabbed by the scruff of the neck.

Hatchet for his part has taken refuge behind the bar from which he is now hurling empty bottles at the rozzers:

"You culchie bastards won't be taking me," he screams at the top of his lungs he's been watching too many gangster films.'

"Here, take this ejit," says the rozzer holding me as he passes me to the Garda holding Redser firmly in his grip. The other two police officers then went about their task of getting Hatchet from behind the bar from where he was still mouthing obscenities and throwing bottles; none of which hit their target. He must think he is Geronimo or is scared out of his wits. He keeps bawling: "You'll never take me, never."

In the meantime Redser and I are taken out to the police car where Jobo is already in the rear seat looking shamefaced. Moments later we three are joined by 'no surrender' Hatchet who has been hauled out from behind the bar by the scruff of his neck; he is still defiantly kicking and screaming.

There are two police cars outside the club so we boys are evenly divided between the two of them. Both Redser and I are squeezed between two giant Garda and I can smell the strong pong of mothballs and stale cigarette smoke from their uniforms. "Right, lads: You're well and truly caught so there'll be no fucking fairy stories when you get to the station."

"Fuck off, you div," Redser says. "We were only walking by and this geezer says do you want to come in and help us arrange the chairs and tables for a function later today. We've done nothing wrong and I want my da at the station, you hear."

"You'll get your da alright," says the driver as we pull into the confines of Store Street Police Station: "No doubt he'll be in Cusack's pub having his drop of the relic."

Separated from Redser I found myself in a room now familiar to me; the room where the table and the chairs are bolted to the floor. There I am confronted by two lethal looking uniformed policemen. "Right, you little fucker," says the bigger of the two: "Tell us about the little robbery sprees you have been on for the last few weeks and no fucking lies as we know all that you have done."

"I don't know what you are talking about." I truthfully tell him. My retort earned me a smack across the back of my head: "Don't be clever, you little shite. I said we know what you have been up to."

"I haven't been up to anything," I snuffle. My ears are ringing in my head from the smack I have just received; snot is running from my nose in rivulets and drops splatter across the table as yet another hand slaps me across the back of my head. The force of the blow shot my head forward so it hit the table's corner; it was then the blood began to spurt.

"You little gobshite," the bigger of the two exclaims angrily: "Now we have got to make a report as to how you fell over and hurt your head."

The smaller of the two policeman said it would be alright as he left the room. By this time I am sobbing; nothing had prepared me for this. It was just as well. Had I anticipated their being so rough I would have shit myself in the police car. My head is throbbing with the pain and I feel sick. Had I had any bravado it has long since evaporated.

"I want my ma, I want my da," I cry piteously. At this point the smaller Garda came back into the room. He is carrying some Jack's roll and a cup of tea. Leaning over he uses a lump of the jack's roll and tries to stem the flow of blood from the wound on my head.

"Drink the tea, lad. Do you want a fag?" The bigger policeman offers a pack of John Players navy cut.

I sobbed that I didn't smoke and I wanted my da my ma. Pushing the cigarette pack towards me he smirks: "You might as well start now as never."

My hand is shaking as I reach out and draw one of the cigarettes from the open packet. As I place the ciggie in my mouth the policeman leans towards me and lights it with a match. As I nervously pulled on the cigarette I started to cough and wretch, which added to my winging and sniveling and only made me feel much worse. The slightly built copper has in the meantime muttered something about my wound having stopped bleeding but my head feels like a kicked football and it throbbing like mad.

"Okay, we're going to write up a statement for you to sign," one of them says. "You can hold on to these he adds as he passes me the cigarettes and box of matches.

His attention is then turned to scribbling down the statement, which claims that all four of us burgled the Town and Muck on two occasions; today and the previous Sunday. As he finishes reading it out to me he pushes it across the table top and glowers: "Sign it!"

"I can't and I will not," I said having found some of my wits. "I was only there today and I cannot sign for the other three." Young as I was I was under no illusions as to my standing in the community if I grassed on my mates.

"Okay! We'll fucking change it then won't we," he snarled with obvious distaste for my poor attempt at rebellion. The revised statement was nearer the truth, but not the truth: It stated simply that I broke into the hall and stole minerals and a money box. Signing it I pushed it back towards him after which I was led out to the front desk to find my ma waiting for me. Her expression tells me she isn't too happy to see me but I am delighted to see her.

Taking one look at my appearance she started to shout at the guards, demanding to know what they have been doing to me. Emphatically she wants to know the reason for my bloodied and bruised head.

"He fell over when he was trying to get away from us," the smaller of the two policemen says without a blink of his lying eye. I gather that is the matter satisfactorily dealt with as they know well that a policeman's version of events counts far higher than that of a slip of a kid. Ma's expression is one of contempt; she clearly doesn't believe a word they say and perhaps rightly believes that one is as bad as the other; me and the policemen. Snatching my hand she wheels around and leads me out of the police station. The police have their man; all in a day's work.

"Why do you do it? You don't have to get in these scrapes and you are never the better off for it' you always end up worse off."

All the way home she keeps repeating herself ranting and raving. Half the time she is talking to me and the rest of it she is talking to herself. All I want to do is get home; my head is throbbing with the pain from the blow and the sweet oblivion of sleep is all I yearn for.

On the following day I looked for the lads and found them but they were in no mood to see me. Each of them are scowling as they watch my approach: "What did you tell the fucking coppers," Redser roars. "I am going to kill you, you little fuckin shite."

"Nothing; I told them nothing," I wailed as I waited for the expected blows to fall. They didn't come but Hatchet's words were as stinging. "They said you were singing like a canary," he grimaced.

"No, no," I cried: "I never said anything about you three. They charged only me for doing the job. They tried to get me for doing both Sundays but I wouldn't do it; I only admitted to this Sunday. I was out with my auntie last Sunday and could prove it."

"Did you plead guilty to it then?"

"I had to," I told Redser. "We were in the fucking Town and Muck when we were grabbed. What was the point in saying I wasn't there?"

"You never plead guilty," he snarled: "Even when you are caught red-handed. Us three have been let go as we're only kids and wouldn't admit to it so you're the ejit that will go away on your own for doing it, you thicko. Now fuck off as we can't be seen with a robber," he added laughing.

His words more than anything else haunted me through the rest of my life; those words expressed the ultimate betrayal and what made it worse was they had betrayed me whilst accusing me of betraying them. It was a lesson learned; that was how friends could treat you. I would look at people in a different light from there on.

My case was due to be heard tomorrow and I was mortified my da wouldn't be able to be there with me. He had just started a new job and there being no way he could take a day off it was once again left to my ma to take me to court. My case was to be heard at the same children's court in Dublin Castle. It was my heartfelt wish that the same judge wouldn't be hearing my case as I still hadn't paid the ten shilling fine from my last appearance.

Despite it being June the rain was coming down in stair rods as we set out; it was nine o'clock and we had to be there for the hour of ten. Ma assured me there was plenty of time: "Get here, under the umbrella," she said. "You'll be getting your good clothes wet." We trotted on our way, ma holding my hand tightly. Little did I know it would be nearly two years before I would again see North Great George's Street?

As we approached the forbidding court buildings with their black soot-laden sandstone blocks I could see a lot of youngsters hanging around outside. Ma pulled me inside the doors and into the hallway to escape the rain outside. Others were crowded in there for the same reason and among them all I could see the bigger of the two policemen who had taken my statement. As soon as he set eyes on ma and me he came over.

As though it was a mere pleasantry exchanged between us he told us that my case should be dealt with by eleven o'clock. Had I but realised what my fate was to be the wait would have been much longer for I would have been out of that court building like a scalded cat.

As we waited for my name to be called a woman emerged from the court room and she was crying piteously: "My poor Jacko. My poor Jacko. He is being sent to Dangein for four years and he is but twelve years old the wee mite. I hope that woman judge rots in hell, the fucking toffee-nosed bitch: Rot in hell for sending children to industrial schools for years. All he was doing was trying to feed his brothers and his sisters, bless him."

"Ma," I wailed: "What is happening? What's Dangein?"

"Shush, son. It's okay. He must have done something really wrong. I noticed ma looked pensive and was biting her bottom lip in anxiety. It was then I heard my name being called out.

We went through the doors; it was the same court and looked exactly the same except this time it smelled of stale clothing. Perhaps it was the affect of the rain sodden clothes people were wearing that morning. As I took my place as directed the female judge peered at me over her rimless glasses. She studied me intensely for a moment as though trying to read my thoughts and guess my background and wasn't looking too kindly at me at all. Turning to the Guard she says in an educated voice: "He has pleaded guilty to the charge laid before him?"

The guard nodded: "Yes, your honour."

"Well now," the judge said as she paused for effect: "This is a most serious case. Does the child have his parents in court?

Again the guard nodded and told the judge my mother was with me as he looked in her direction.

"Step up, madam," her honour calls to mother. As my ma respectfully stood in the dock beside me the judge addressed her directly: "Can you explain to the court how your son happens to be growing up the way he is? Do you not have any control over him, and where is the child's father?"

My ma tried to explain that I got into the wrong company and that I am easily led but I have promised her faithfully I will never play with the boys' again and the unfortunate lapse will never be repeated. She went on to explain firmly that my da was working; it was a new job and it wasn't possible for him to take the time off to attend court.

Turning again to the guard standing beside me the judge asked if I had form. He replied that I had and that I have an outstanding fine yet to be paid. I stood there shaking as they talked about me: I had no excuses to make but in mitigation I was only twelve-years old.

She addressed me directly: "I sentence you to Letterfrack Industrial School. There you will remain until you are sixteen-years old." Immediately she had spoken she turned to ask the court clerk if I might be taken the same day. Rummaging through a few papers on her desk the clerk replied all was in order for me to do so. With that I was taken away and hadn't the slightest idea what was going on.

As I disappear I can hear my ma pleading for leniency: "Please, he is only a child can't you see. Give him a chance; he won't do it again, your honour." The judge sternly rebuked ma; telling her the case was over and for her to remove herself from the court.

"Next case," the clerk shouts as I am taken out of the courtroom to another room situated at the rear of the building. Ominously it has a heavy steel door and has a barred window set too high to be of any use to me. Inside are two other kids about the same age as I am. Looking around I take in the bare green walls. Inside I am collapsing; I haven't the faintest idea what is going on. One of the other two children is crying whilst the other is looking nervous whilst he pulls on a cigarette.

"What did you get," he says looking directly at me.

"Three years and six months I think," I told him as he looked at me coolly.

"You jammy bollix," he says: "I've got four years in Dangein and yer man here has got a month in Marlborough House."

"Will I be able to see me ma?"

"Don't know. They wouldn't let me see mine."

I am overwhelmed by anxiety. I want to burst into tears as the other child is doing but being eleven years old I feel I must show some self restraint. I have a terrible sick sensation in the pit of my stomach. I can't stop myself from shivering but it is through nerves, not cold. Oh God! What is to become of me? I was terrified. Will I ever see my family again; where is Letterfrack? My mind is just a chaotic jumble of questions that cannot be answered. Amidst it all I keep wordlessly repeating to myself I must whatever happens be strong, I must be strong.

The other child has stopped his crying and from somewhere I can hear my ma calling my name over and over again. "Son. Son can you hear me? It's alright, son; it is okay. I will write to you. You will be alright. Be strong be brave you will be alright"

"I know, ma," I call back. "I will be alright." Thank goodness she cannot see me for I am still trembling and wanting to be sick my stomach is churning in terror. But I remind myself, I am not a baby any more and I will stick up for myself. Today and from here on I am an eleven-year old man. Such were my thoughts when I heard again my name being called; this time by a guard.

I was led outside to the police car and looking around there's no sign of my ma at all. She must have gone on home. The rain has eased off a little but the skies are heavy and leaden and there's a chill in the air.

"In the back, boyo," the Garda officer says as he opens the car's rear door. The seat seems so big; he must hardly be able to see the small boy huddled in its corner. It seems neither of the boys in the cell is going with me. Before the door has clunked shut I am already planning my escape: I will be straight out of there at the first set of traffic lights. It is then I notice the doors have no door handlers on the inside. Fuck! There is no way out.

"Well, my boyo," the officer says. "You will be having a lovely time where you are going. You will be cutting hay, digging up the bog. You will also learn to read and write, and how to use a knife and fork." He seems amused by his own wit.

The big mutton head I am thinking how would he know what type of a time I am going to have? How would he know what I am about to endure.

As the car speeds along it passes the Guinness Brewery at St James' Gate. I have no idea where I am being taken but I am sure to find out soon. In no time at all the police car pulls up outside Kingsbridge Railway Station; a big imposing building. As the Garda comes around to open the car's rear door he warns me against doing anything stupid as he takes me firmly by my arm.

"We are going to meet someone who will take you by train to Galway," he says as we enter the huge ticket hall where by the office I can see another guard. As we approach him I see he is a much older; a grey-haired man with a pot belly. He too is wearing the uniform of the Garda and has a raincoat draped over his arm. He is also carrying a brown leather box with a handle on it.

"Only the one today?"

"Sure; no bother at all," says the policeman who brought me here from Dublin Castle as he produces a sheet of paper for him to acknowledge 'custody of the body.' I am not dead yet I am thinking to myself as the first guard walks off whistling a merry tune.

"Now, my bucko," my new guard says to me: "We have quite a long journey ahead of us today and it is best for you to know you can make it easy or hard for yourself."

I have no idea what he is talking about. He then asks if I want to use the lavatory, saying we have a few minutes to spare. I nod silently.

"You need to poo or pee? I will come with you."

"No, just a piss, sir."

"A piss you say; there'll be none of that kind of language," he muttered as the back of his hand slapped my head. The tears well up at his unnecessary harshness but I was determined not to cry. He was standing right behind me as I did a wee. "Shake it, lad; shake it now."

The walk along the railway platform seemed endless and the train itself seemed to be as long. My guardian seemed to be looking for a carriage that was empty and eventually he found one. Telling me to make myself comfortable he took a newspaper from the box he was carrying.

I am sat up against the window with him sitting right next to me, barring the way to the door and freedom. Anyway, I am jammed in by the small table in front of us. Any chance of fleeing goes out of the window as the train pulls away and the station platform slips by quicker and quicker. I have been on a train just once before; that was when we went to Balbriggan for our summer holidays with the Religious society.

As the train gathers speed I gaze at the passing landscape without giving it too much thought. I am trying to concentrate; hoping for the best whilst willing myself to be strong in the face of anything. How things can change so quickly: it was only hours since I slept in my bed and breakfasted with my brothers and sisters. Now I was in a train with a strange man not knowing where I was going or if I would ever see my family again.

Placing my crossed arms on the table I lay my head on them and giving in to exhaustion was soon fast asleep. I later awoke to the sound of squealing brakes, metal set against metal and a juddering from the train as it pulled to a halt. Shaking my head I wondered where we were as the guard asked me if I wanted a cup of tea. I nodded that I did then followed him out to the crowded café on the station platform. I was conscious of the stares our presence was generating; a boy with a policeman.

"Two teas, two Ham sandwiches," he says to the lady serving at the counter. After paying he added sugar to my own cup and carried our lunch back to the compartment. More passengers have joined our train and there are people in our compartment now. When I take my seat I stare at the lady sitting opposite to us. She looks elegant; a bit posh and has fox furs around her neck even though it's summer. Clearly seen are the fox's claws and on view too the needles piercing her hair. Her suit is plaid and she carries a large black handbag, which is a contrast to her flame-red lipstick. My guard acknowledges her with a nod that is returned by a faint smile.

Sipping my tea and nibbling my sandwich I listen to the clackety-clack of the train's wheels as it picks up speed: "Where would you be taking the young lad?" asks the lady passenger.

"He is a juvenile delinquent," he says: "I am taking him to Galway and from there he will be taken to Letterfrack an Industrial School that is for his type."

She looked at me with a mixture of compassion and curiosity: "And by the looks of him you wouldn't think butter would melt in his mouth," she says. Silly woman, I think to myself: Now what exactly would I be doing with butter in my mouth? Mean time the two of them keep up their conversation about the weather and the country in general, which concerns me not at all. I am off into a childish reverie and my thoughts largely centre on; I am in the shit; how do I get out of this mess and get home again?

After what seemed to be a long time we pair arrive at Galway station. Saying his goodbyes to the chance encounter he takes me, not ungentle by the arm: "Okay, boyo. There's not long to go now and if you're having any ideas about running forget them."

Ten minutes later and we were traipsing down the corridor of a Gardai station. It is an old building and its mustiness evokes centuries of usage. Behind the reception desk a florid faced policeman seemingly awaiting our arrival.

"Hello; is this the lad we're expecting; the one for the bog?"

"The one and the same," says my uniformed companion to which the policeman gruffly responded by lifting the counter lid to allow me through: "I will look after him until the brothers arrive."

"Brothers I wonder what are Brothers"? I will quickly find out.

As he glanced at me thoughtfully I tried reading his thoughts but they were impenetrable. I sat and watched silently as he took the sheet of paper from my former custodian who asked the policeman to sign it.

Then, with a cheery salute he went on his way having explained he had no wish to miss the train home. At least he is going home thought I. God alone knew where my home was going to be.

The uncle-like policeman offered me a chair and it is a relief to know I am not in gaol as such; I am not locked in but there is nowhere for me to go to anyway. There's little for me to do but to sit forlornly behind the counter as the policeman turns his back on me and scribbles away at some paperwork. On the far wall there are some presses with a long table beneath each of them. I can't help but notice the paintwork is bilious green and peeling.

"You want a cup of tea, lad?" He asks after a while.

The policeman lights his pipe and studies me as he asks his question. Nodding my head I silently mouthed, 'yes please.' I couldn't help but wonder at what was going on in his head. Did he have children; perhaps a son my age? He has a gas ring from which I can hear a comforting sound; it has already bought the kettle to the boil or rather its singing. It is a whistling kettle and when the boiling water is added to the tin cup its contents look as dark as Guinness it's so strong.

"You'll want milk and sugar I suppose," says the policeman. I notice the three stripes on his arm but can only guess at his rank; I think to myself that he isn't an ordinary copper. As I watch in silence he pours a little milk into the cup and then taking an old jam jar near filled with sugar he adds two spoons before stirring the brew. His tea is as thick as stew but I daren't say anything that might be interpreted as being ungracious.

"Here you are, son. Get this down you. You'll need it after that long journey. His words brought me back to thinking about the distance that lay between me and my Dublin home; I might just as well have been on the dark side of the moon.

"You'll be wanting to go to the lav' then? The brothers will be here to collect you soon and it is quite a long drive where you are going. Without waiting for me to reply he ushered me out to the station's backyard. The smell is something else and something I will never get used to. I try to hold my breath while I am pissing but the stench will stay with me; becoming a part of the fabric of my clothing. There will be no easy escape from it. Nor will there be any escape from where I am destined. But I am not to know that at this time.

Outside I could hear a car pulling up against a backdrop of dogs barking. This is followed by what I come to know as a Christian Brother entering the police station, peering around as he did so. God help us but Christian brothers they were most certainly not. He is of average size with grey hair trimmed short; clean shaven and with a portly belly wearing a black cassock and a priest's dog collar his dark eyes examine me.

"Is this the one then?" He asks the Garda.

"It is, brother. And if you will kindly sign for him you can soon be on your way."

I felt as a slave must have felt as my guardianship changed hands from the uniformed police office to the cassock-wearing brother. The paperwork signed and with a curtly recognition of my presence he ushered me out to his car, telling me as he did so that we had a fair drive ahead of us.

"Best of luck to you, bucko," I hear the guard say as I exit the police station door. In the street outside is the brother's estate car. I recall it was a bright evening and as I climbed into the car's backseat I heard its door slamming shut behind me. This time I am not on my own; in the rear of the car, separated by wire mesh are two large dogs they are Irish red setters.

"Be a good lad and they won't bite you," says the Christian Brother. His reassurances carried little weight.

I had never been so close to such large dogs before and neither of them looked very friendly. Such was my predicament as the car made its way out of Galway City and from there on drove along narrow country lanes bordered by hand-built stone walls on either side. The land was ever so green and conscious of the two hounds in the back as they balefully looked at me I tried to read their thoughts.

Was I merely a curiosity or a new member of the pack? For some reason I noticed the absence of trees.

There were many sheep in the fields and we occasionally passed stone cottages set a little back from the road. I don't recall seeing villages; only occasional smallholdings and cottages. At no point in the journey did the brother speak to me; not a pleasantry nor anything to suggest his being curious as to me as a person or my reason for being there. I was in a dream world but hardly a pleasant one as I idly wondered what awaited me. By now the two dogs had settled down and were asleep.

Rounding a bend I could now see a large imposing fortress-like building and thought that at last we had reached our destination. It looked like a castle but I later learned it was Kylemore Abbey, a private school for girls. A further half hour passed before we reached a village and it was there that the brother swung the wheel as we turned up a small lane.

I could make out some buildings over on my right; we drove until we ran out of lane and then pulling hard on the handbrake we came to a stop. Welcome to Letterfrack thought I to myself.

As we stepped out of the car another brother of the order approached us. There was still daylight and from where I stood in the chill evening air I could see we were on the top west side of a square. There was a row of neat cottages running behind us to the east, and a big yard overlooked by two grim buildings; one to its left and the other straight ahead. On my right was a high wall and a smaller building.

The approaching brother was again smallish. I couldn't help but notice the blackness of his hair and his pointy chin. He was also wearing a black cassock with dog collar and his hands were buried deep under his brother's cassock. It was this brother who led me trough a doorway and around the side of the building to what was a very big kitchen.

"There is some bread and milk for you, child. Eat it up as you will not be getting any more this side of morning."

The milk was in a tin mug; the bread was in the shape of a small loaf and the butter was there but without a knife with which to spread it. Breaking the bread in half I simply slapped the butter in between the two halves and wolfed it down whilst gulping the milk. I hadn't realised just how hungry I was; the last I had eaten was the sandwich on the train.

The brother waited patiently, watching me with some interest until I had finished the meal. Only then did he instruct me to follow him and so off we went, into a yard across it and through a door, we climbed a flight of stairs and from there into a washroom.

There my clothing was removed and I stood there naked as he handed me a nightshirt, a towel and a toothbrush. "Wash and clean your teeth," was all he muttered.

Having done as I was told he then took me through a door into a dormitory that was filled with what looked like endless rows of beds. Soon I found myself standing next to a bed on the right side of the hall situated about a third of the way up from the door to the washroom.

"This is where you now sleep."

I could see the bedclothes were all neatly folded at one end of the bed. "Make your bed now and go to sleep." He said

Disappearing through a door at the top of the dormitory I could see a light flicker trough where I could see a hatch of sorts. Making my bed I felt as miserable as could be imagined; especially when I again heard the mocking echoes of Redser, Jobo and Hatchet's voices. As I lay in empty loneliness I was thinking of the day's cruel series of events; not the least the callousness of the presiding judge. I filled up but fought back the tears as I pulled the sheet up to my chin.

Somewhere in the gloom I could hear the sounds made by other boys who were sleeping; light snores and snuffles and the occasionally creaking of a bed when a boy moved restlessly in his sleep. But not a whisper of welcome did I hear. I tried to sleep but there was too much on my mind. I instinctively felt I was at the beginning of a heartbreaking journey and wondered how I was going to manage my way through it.

Chapter 5

"Wake up, you shower. Wake up!" The sharply spoken commands were accompanied by much clapping of hands. Jerking awake I ask myself what is going on; I feel as though I have been asleep for just an hour or so. Beyond my bedclothes I can make out the brother tramping up and down the dormitory constantly clapping his hands and barking, wake up. He is the same one who directed me to my bed the previous evening.

"Stand by your beds, all of you," he shouts. I half step, half fall out of my own bed then realising I am on the wrong side of it I scramble over to its furthest side. From somewhere behind me I can hear sniggering and glancing over my shoulder I see a big lad with jet black hair chuckling. He recognises I am new. Further up the line of beds the brother is coming nearer and nearer, placing his hand under the sheets of each blanket as he approaches.

He is looking for wet beds and seeming to know where he is looking it isn't long before he finds one.

Nausea swept over me at the sound of the perfunctory slaps that rain down on the hapless boy's head and face. These are followed up by a kick at the lad's backside. My shoulders hunched with revulsion as the child fell to the floor wailing and crying.

"You dirty little pissy bastard," the brother screams at the figure hunched on the bare floor: "How dare you piss your bed; how dare you?"

"I'm sorry, brother," the youngster sobs: "I thought it was only a bad dream I was having."

"Dream? Dream you say? I'll give you dream," yells the brother fuming with incandescent rage. "Fold your bed and dry your sheets."

Each holding our breath we waited as the brother commenced checking each of the beds for a telltale sign of dampness but he found no others. Reaching my bed he glares at me: "I don't want any more pissy beds: Do you understand me? Now go and wash."

Welcome to hell I thought.

This then was clearly the way the Christian Brothers dealt with boy problems; with slaps, oaths, anger, fists and kicks. Under no illusions I realised I had to learn quickly but cautiously. I held back whilst the other boys used the wash basins; I knew my place in the pecking order and had no desire to upset anyone. The ritual afterwards was to get ourselves dressed, return to our beds and to stand by them.

From where I was standing I could see the bed had been pissed in, which was still unmade. The covers had been folded back over the bed's end and the sheets stretched out so they could dry better; they would not be changed for fresh bedding.

By nightfall they would be dry but carry the smell of the previous night's involuntary bedwetting.

"Okay. All of you in a straight line."

The order was broken by chattering. Whack! A smack descended on the head of the lad seen talking: "Don't speak before line-out in the yard, you fucker," the brother shrieks. The brother's name I later find out is Chinney.

Following the other boys as they troop silently down the stairway to the yard I see another group emerging from the same door who then form a line behind us. A head count takes place and in rows of two we walk up to the church.

This is to be 7.30am mass and will be a daily ritual come rain, hail or snow. We boys take our places in the pews to the left of the church facing the altar. The villagers from the surrounding areas are on the right of us. During the week there are only a few elderly ladies present but on Sunday that side of the small church filled to capacity.

After mass we again filed down to the yard in a two-abreast column and on getting there I learn that we can sit around and talk among ourselves. I was instantly approached by two lads who seem welcoming. I wasn't sure what they meant when one of them told me I would be alright here; the brothers like the pretty ones they said as they walked away sniggering. I was soon to find out what they meant.

Once again there was a loud clapping of hands and it seemed to me that this was more often done than hands being held together in prayer.

This time it is a well-built brother who reminds us all of Friar Tuck. He is rotund though hardly jovial with patches of dark wispy hair pulled over his balding head.

Okay," he shouts. "Form a line; you know the drill."

We did so and again in a column we disappeared into the dining hall, which is through the same main doors leading to the stairway and to the dormitories but set off to the left on the ground floor. I feel the gaze of Friar Tuck:

"You wait, boy. You will be shown to your place so just stand to the side and wait."

As soon as the others found their places at their table and stood silently at them the brother took me to the first table on the left nearest to the kitchen door and places me at the inside head of it with my back to a window.

"Grace." He barked to the assembled lines of youngsters.

The lads having given the Lord thanks for what they were about to eat immediately began to chat among themselves; a bedlam punctuated by the sharp scraping of chair legs on bare floorboards.

Set before each of us are mugs of tea; a bowl of porridge and bread. The boys fall on the fare ravenously, each trying to talk to their mates as they wolf their breakfasts down. I gazed around my table but look in vain for a face that might be familiar to me. I am starved and my plate is soon lick-clean; I have no idea when I will next eat. Once again I am plucked out by Friar Tuck.

"You'll be working with me today, boy." He says without any friendliness in his voice.

Outside in the yard there is a set of scaffolding adjacent to the outside walls of the building. The entire apparatus is on wheels so it will be mobile; able to be shunted along the walls from task to task.

By the time the boys have dispersed, Friar Tuck turns to me and tells me to start climbing. He tells me we will be painting the guttering.

I am terrified of heights; I often have nightmares in which I am falling from insecure heights and have never before been as high as the eaves of the roof. From up there I can see sheep grazing in the nearby fields and in the distance a solitary man with his dog. My legs are shaking like jelly;

my nervousness isn't helped by the apparent shakiness of the scaffolding, which I can only hope is secure. The brother can see I am so terrified I am likely to be useless at the tasks he has in mind for me.

"Are you alright, lad? You look sickly; pale."

"I am terrified of heights." I tell him.

"Sure, you will get used to it," he says. "The best way to do that is just to get your mind off it by painting the guttering.

You're a load of fucking bollix I think to myself. I'll paint your fucking head if you keep me up here much longer. By this time I am trying my best to wield the paintbrush but my hands and legs are shaking with anxiety. There's a light wind which moves the scaffolding adding to my nervousness. To me the breeze seems like a tempest: I cannot stay up here; I am scared shitless.

Hearing my words he tells me I will be scared if I get the feel of his hand and tells me that I am up here for the day. I was left in no doubt that I had no choice but to grin and bear it and from that day to this my fear of heights has remained.

The experience wasn't something to allay my fears. Friar Tuck was hardly the worst of the brothers it was all still tough on a child so young.

We later stopped for lunch taken in the dining room where again I was directed to the same place as I had my breakfast. On this occasion we were given bread with jam, and a mug of tea. The room was quite empty though as most of the boys were working either at the farm or they were at the bog. Those who shared the tables with me had been working in the tailoring shop; as carpenters, in the laundry or on general maintenance work as I was. A few of the others were attending school.

Lunch over I returned to the scaffold. The wind having dropped a little failed to alleviate my nervousness. I was given to understand, instinctively and by example the brothers' policy was to break the boys' spirits so they would become compliant with the regime. This they believed would make us men, like them. I hoped not.

They were nothing other than an assemblage of sick perverts only too quick to abuse the power they held and to turn a blind eye; cover up for their accomplices in sin.

It has been said that not all of the brothers were wicked; there must have been some good ones who were driven by the ideals of their calling. This was not based on my experience. Furthermore, Letterfrack was a close community and no brother or lay person who worked at St Joseph's or lived in the village could honestly say they were unaware of the abuses that were prevalent there.

Such abuses occurred on a daily basis, were routine and random. There was no one; person or authority to which a child could turn to. The Christian Brothers had a free hand in an isolated region and knowing it they abused it. After work you went to the jacks to wash your hands after which you went to the yard to wait until teatime. The same routine was followed day in and day out. Two single files would form and the column would then disappear into the dining hall. All meals were bread based; the youngsters were fed to the extremes of asceticism.

After supper, if the weather was fine the boys would go into the yard until bedtime; if the weather was poor then it was the hall. The custom was, early to bed, early to rise will make the brothers wealthy but never wise.

*   *   *

I dreamed a great deal; it was a form of nocturnal escapism from the constant threat posed by the brothers and the unrelenting ritual of work and conformity to prison-like procedures. During one such night I dreamt of a time when I was six-years old. It was when we lived at Sandymount and in my dream I visualised my da returning home the worse for drink. Then too I had been asleep but it was his screaming at my ma that had woken me up.

"I will fucking kill you; I will chop your fucking head off and you will be running around this room like a headless chicken, you bitch."

Neither of them noticed me as I stood there in the doorway trying to make sense of what was happening. My ma was screaming back at him, reminding him that he had left us no money for food or for anything else; we were destitute.

"How are we supposed to live at all when you are drinking and gambling our money away? There is no money to pay the rent and feed the children? I am leaving; I can't stand this anymore. I am not coming back."

It was then my da saw me standing at the door: ""Fuck off then, and take that little brat with you," he snarled.

"Oh God; please be to God; leave the child out of it will you? Come here, son," she said to me. "I will get you dressed."

Turning on my father she called him a bastard and told him to leave the house immediately; that he was a disgrace who should be ashamed of himself. He set his jaw: "I am going nowhere. You get the fuck out now."

Dressing me quickly my ma takes my hand and we leave our home, pulling the door shut behind us. I am the only child at home at this stage as the others are in a home for a couple of weeks. Outside it is very dark and raining. I ask my ma where we are going. She tells me we will be going to grannies' to see if we can stay with her.

A long walk is ahead of us with my ma holding tightly on to my hand. As we walk through the darkened streets of Sandymount, Irish Town and on to Ringsend I am doing my best to stay warm and dry but it is futile; the rain is persistent and the night air cold. With my hand firmly held I had little choice but to keep up with ma as we made our way along the river and towards Ringsend Park Cottages.

This is where my Grannie live's with her man. I know him only as Ned and not as granda, which I find a little confusing. This isn't helped by my uncle and aunt also living there with them.

It seems several minutes pass between ma rapping with the door knocker and the light going on inside. I can hear grandma calling who's there. "It's me," my ma replies through the letterbox. Moments later the door opens and my grandma is standing there. She has long white hair and has pulled about herself a long dark housecoat.

"What on earth is wrong," she says as she peers at the pair of us on the darkened doorstep glistening in the rain. "What do you want at this hour?"

"It's himself," my ma replies: "He is at it again. I had to run off with the lad before he killed the both of us."

"Well you can't stay here. We told you about him time after time but would you listen?"

"Please, please," my ma is pleading: "If only for the lad's sake. It is raining and we are both freezing. We can't go back. You wouldn't see us on the streets; not on a night like this.

We can sit in a chair. Anything, we can't go back."

"No, you can't stop here. You made your bed, you lie on it. We told you not to marry him but you always knew better." With that she closed the door in our faces. We pair just stood there helpless. There was very little help in Ireland at this time for battered or abused wives. Mother was desperately searching for a solution; we had to seek shelter from somewhere. Suddenly she remembered a friend who might help. The rain was relentless and by now we are both soaked to the skin and shivering as we retraced our footsteps to Irishtown and to where my ma's friend lives her name is Sheila and she has been friends with ma for as long as I can remember, she was a lovely woman and a great friend to me ma.

She was really nice when we finally reached her home. She had immediately come to the door as soon as she heard ma's knocking. "What's wrong," she says looking us both up and down. "Is it his nibs again?"

My ma silently nods her head before saying: "Yes, and it is getting worse."

We are both ushered in and I am taken to the bathroom where I am quickly dried and warmed, put into pajamas and placed under a blanket on the settee where I am soon fast asleep. Hours later I was taken to see some people. I was afterwards placed in the orphanage from which I was to later escape only to be betrayed to the Garda when I arrived at the wrong auntie's home.

But now I am in the Letterfrack industrial school and along the rows of beds hidden in the darkness I listen to the other boys snoring, their dreaming sounds; the occasional cough or fart. The windows are bare of curtains and through them I can see the light of the moon shining on our small patch of the earth.

Tossing and turning, my thoughts filled with the past and the uncertainties of the future sleep just will not come. As soon as I start to drift off a boy's coughing brings me back to consciousness. I wonder how many other boys are lying there in the darkness listening to the same sounds.

What is going trough their minds I can only wonder.

"Fuck this," I think to myself: "I will never get to sleep this night."

As soon as my thoughts settle the brother known as Chinney emerges from his room and begins to scream at the boy. "Swallow it; swallow it, you bastards. Stop coughing it up. You'll wake everyone up."

The brother had already done that with his screaming and those he woke up must have been bewildered by his words and temperament.

But little did I know they were used to it.

This was a regular occurrence.

"If I have to come back in then it will be the end of you," he curses. "Swallow it or else." His words are followed by the sound of a slap on the child's head. This particular brother I later discover was a particularly notorious individual yet he was in charge of the dormitory that was to be my home for the next three and a half years. I tried to imagine how long three and a half years might be by thinking back that far: I had been eight years old then and that seemed a lifetime ago. Eventually I fell asleep.

Clap! Clap! Clap! "Get up, all of you." A sound that would echo through my life from those mornings when we were woken by Chinney. Afraid of what might happen if I formed friendships with others I had decided I would keep my own company as much as possible.

I hadn't forgotten Redser's betrayal had put me here in the industrial school. The other boys had their problems; And God knows I had my own.

The first week passed me by. Much of it was spent on the scaffolding leaving me even more frightened of heights than before. I was petrified by the Sunday when we went to mass. There were more parishioners in their pews on the day of worship. Sitting opposite the villagers looked very grand in the finery but to compensate we too had suits to wear. The younger girls among the folk sitting opposite would shyly look across at us boys and giggle to themselves. At the end of the service the priest would detail the donations made by each.

"Butcher, one and sixpence; farmer sixpence," and so on. If the weather was good we would be taken for a walk along the main road but never through the village. It gave a great sense of freedom if one was picked to go on the walk, even though we had no idea at all in what part of Ireland we were now living. The only clue was that it took a day to get here.

Sometimes we would walk in a double line which gave opportunity to chat with whichever companion we found ourselves sharing the walk with. Not everyone was talkative though; some were withdrawn. Perhaps they had problems communicating or were afraid of feeling the hand or boot of one of the brothers.

On Mondays the dreary routine started all over again with clap, clap and more clap, clap until we were each on our feet sharpish and standing beside our beds; a line of obedient little serfs. Then it was church followed by breakfast. The work from the scaffold had come to an end and so I was placed in the school. I found myself in a room on the ground floor facing out towards the front gate and the main road. There were about twenty-five of us in this classroom: The brother in charge seemed younger than were the others.

Occasionally the brothers were changed to suit themselves whilst on occasion, presumably to allow freedom for some, brothers would cover for others whilst attending to their own waifs.

One of these Christian Brothers was known to be a bit of a lunatic. He always carried with him a leather strap that had lead stitched into it. This was about a half inch thick and perhaps sixteen inches long with a grip for the hand carved into it.

I often wondered who made these leathers for the brothers. Who was the manufacture of these lethal weapons that were used on young boys to inflict so much pain and suffering?

When he was using it on a boy the child would be required to hold his hand open and upwards about twelve-inches above the brother's desk. Raising the strap as far back over his shoulder as he could reach this brother would then bring it down with as much force as he could muster. This meant the unfortunate child's hand when struck would slam against the desk top; a technique that resulted in the victim's hand receiving a double injury accompanied by excruciating pain. The searing pain was described correctly as like having grasped a red hot poker. Often, as we were studying he would stride up and down between the rows of desks and for no apparent reason slap the boys on their legs or hands; he just enjoyed doing so. Many a boy ended the day's schooling covered in welts and bruises.

Another punishment was to make a child face the wall. This often happened when the brother thought he had inflicted enough pain and the child had taken as much physical punishment as he could with the leather. Often the boy would be ordered to kneel facing the wall rather than just stand with his back to the class. There was rarely a reason for his doing so; the ordeal was randomly inflicted.

Luckily for me I could read and write by the time I was placed in the school but many of the other lads could not. Sadly they left the school as illiterate as the day they arrived. Their sole purpose in being at Letterfrack was to serve the brothers and the state and not to be educated.

I recall the day I was required to work on a written composition, the theme of which was to be a storm. So far I had penned: "A tidal wave had come in from the sea and washed away all the stones . . ." As the brother was passing my desk he paused to peer over my shoulder, to better see what had been so far written.

"Tidal wave! Tidal wave?" he screeched at the top of his voice. "There's no such thing as a tidal wave, you idiot. Get to the top of the class."

Tearing my work into strips his eyes bulged with fury as he kept calling me an idiot. He then firmly gripped my wrist so my left hand was held aloft over the desk and beat it until all sensation of feeling left it. I was then forced to my knees, facing the wall, where I was to remain for the rest of the day. It seemed my crime was to use my own imagination and initiative something that was frowned upon; freedom of thought put the fear of God in them. They wanted unthinking robots. We were not there to be taught or to learn only to obey there every whim.

There was no one to turn to for comfort or justice and so we had no reason to believe that there was another world out there. The school's regime was for us normal and we had nothing to compare it with. I had committed crime and this was my punishment and I thought it was normal.

Obviously, with the establishment being so isolated and far from our homes we couldn't expect visits; the only form of communication was by post.

I often received comforting letters from my ma and in many of the letters there was a little money for sweets. I was too smart to tell her what was going on at the school as letters were left open for the brothers to read. Woe betides any child who spoke the truth and in doing so was deemed to have lied. We had reached the stage where we thought the vicious regime was normal for boys who had been badly behaved. Having said that, not all of the children there were delinquents; many were orphans or simply placed there due to family breakdown.

As I was slightly built I was placed in the tailoring shop but the job lasted just about two days.

Perhaps it was because I had accidentally stitched my finger causing blood to appear on the cloth. This brought yet another beating before I was sent to the kitchen.

The kitchen was the responsibility of a balding and very corpulent brother who wore glasses and was somewhat portly, behind his back, we called him Mutton Head. There in the kitchens I would endlessly mop, clean floors and surfaces and peel vegetables. I remember it was about my third day in there when, mopping up the dining room, I thought I heard a whimpering sound coming from an area outside the main door. This was under the stairs where the sweet shop was when it was open. Nervous but curious I eased the door open and peered around the door's jam. There in plain view I could see Mutton Head standing rigid with his back to the wall. Having pulled his cassock back I watched sickened as I saw the reason for the whimpering. A young lad, with the brother's hand on the back of his head, was sucking the Brother's erect penis. I slowly closed the door, horrified and shocked at the spectacle I had witnessed. Although I was sexually unaware at my age, as it was not considered in Ireland to teach sex education in schools and you only learned on the street or by friends, I instinctively knew what was going on was very wrong.

Naturally I thought such practices, like the beatings, might be routine in nature and was sickened by the thought of doing as that boy was made to do.

I didn't of course have anyone to tell what I had seen but I wouldn't have done so anyway; I could well imagine the beating I would have got had I been caught grassing the brother. Frozen with trepidation I continued to mechanically mop the floor and prayed the brother would never come near me. I immediately started to plan my escape from the kitchen job as I hadn't seen this brother work anywhere else at the prison-school. I knew I had to be elsewhere to be safe from his clutches.

As my dining hall place was at the top of the table I started a row with a big lad who sat to my right. Much bigger than I was he had a bit of a mouth on him and was from Limerick. I began to taunt him about his being a wet head which earned me a slap in the face.

That was all I needed.

Grasping the table I flung it and its contents over. As the crashing sound died down a sickening silence descended on the dining room. Everyone was in awe. The poor Limerick lad ran through the doors and into the kitchen with me screaming like a banshee in his wake. I found the lad quivering with fear under one of the kitchen sinks but as I did so Mutton Head caught up with me and lifted me into the air, kicking and screaming my wrath.

Kicking him as hard as I could I screamed my protestations but he wasn't listening. I thought to myself; you won't mess with me, you fucker. I kept on screaming my pent up rage and feared I was changing into some kind of nutter. I had really lost it and was in full hot-blooded rebellion regardless of the consequences.

From here on I was going to fight them and their rotten system; either I would break them or they would break me; there would be no compromise with these evil bastards. Even if they killed me I knew they wouldn't break my spirit.

Hauled from the kitchen by the perspiring cursing Christian Brother I was beaten black and blue. The blows and kicks rained down on me until finally I was dragged back into the dining room, forced to face the wall until everyone else had finished their supper. The repast over we all went into the other hall as it was raining outside.

At no stage was I ever checked out to see to what extent I had been hurt; I was of little concern to them; compassion was as empty as was their souls. I was no more than a piece of meat in an abattoir. As soon as I had been brought to this place of the damned I ceased to exist as a human being, in my own thoughts too. The soulful part of my life was gone; left behind in Dublin. I did at least achieve my aim; I was sacked forthwith from the kitchen. From tomorrow I would be working on the farm and my days were going to start earlier than did the dawn.

They did and the first light often found me sat on a dairymaid's stool, bucket in front of me relieving the animal of its milk. From time to time the beast would kick the bucket, not literally of course and much of one's labors appeared as a pool of milk. The department head was a lay person: Tall and slim he was the son of the head farmer and had the habit of wearing a coat that made him look like an

18th century gentleman. He didn't carry a leather strap but did carry a big cane stick; useful for slapping his Wellington boots as he did his rounds. We knew that when the milk was spilled a cane across the legs would remind us of our clumsiness and so I did all I could to keep out of the way of the cane.

I quickly became adept at manipulating a cow's teat and could deftly twist and squirt the milk straight into my mouth.

This was refreshing though it was body warm; a pleasant enough distraction too. As milking started long before breakfast and we were starving with an hour or so still to go it alleviated my hungriness.

After breakfast it was necessary for us to return to the farm buildings and give them a thorough cleaning. During the summer the cattle would be put out to graze; in the winter confined to the sheds.

It always amazed me how they would walk in a soldier-straight line as they exited or arrived back at the milking sheds. I was now picking up a new career as a farmer. Sure, it was going to be a lot of use to me when I returned to the Irish Republic's capital city; the nearest blade of grass being that at Phoenix Park. The advantage of being with the farm animals was it was rare for one to hurt me and if it did it was unintentional.

Farm work meant long hours of work; animal husbandry doesn't work to a clock and my labors were taking their toll on me. I was twelve now but exceedingly skinny; puny was perhaps the right word to describe me. There was never a break in the climate for winter or summer there was a cold clamminess about the place.

It was having such an effect on my health I became a frequent visitor to the doctor for whatever remedy she thought most suitable.

The doctor was an older woman who lived in the cottage facing the small lake; it was just up the road near to the farm itself. Her surgery was situated along the hall between the classroom and the cloakroom.

I thought her being a woman she would be more compassionate towards us kids but her impartiality was such that she might just as easily have known what was going on. In fact, as she was the one who dealt with excessive injuries and chose never to enquire as to their cause I could only think of her as being complicit, even if only by turning a blind eye.

The only thing that could be said in her favour was that she was never hurtful towards me or as far as I know the other children. It was however a dereliction of duty for she was the one person who would have been listened to by authority had she expressed concern. She chose not to.

One day I was too ill to be at work and was just moping aimlessly when coming down the stairs from the dormitory I see the door to the sweet shop is open; there's not a brother to be seen.

Cautiously I crept inside to find myself in an Aladdin's cave of confectionary. Grabbing three bars of Cleves Toffees I quickly shoved them inside my shirt and legged it into the washrooms. Oh my God; this was all my birthdays in one; how I was going to savour them.

Having hidden the bars in the jacks I crept back up to the stairs and into my bed, relishing the thought of having got one over on the brothers. I was still there when after the day's work was over and the lads returned from the fields they asked me where I had been. I told them I was excused work because I was sick.

"Well it's lucky for you; you weren't at the farm today as Titch was screaming your name.

He was going berserk and was kicking out at kids in all directions while screaming your name. Titch was the brother who had taken over from Big Foot on the farm; Big Foot a brother who had given me many a good kicking but was not as bad as others. Titch was a skinny little fucker and he clearly thought that beating shit out of a kid made him some sort of equal to Big Foot.

It was a wrong calculation as there was the time when, working at the bog I stood up to him. Only a minute beforehand he had beaten me black and blue.

Today, I hadn't the faintest idea why he had been screaming for me. I did see him later in the evening but he passed without saying a word. I never did get to find out why he had wanted me; maybe that was just as well.

Soon my strength was beginning to return and I was put back into the sheds and again milking the cows.

Winter was coming on; here there was constant mist, everything was damp and the chill was constantly in the air. When the normal routine had been met the brothers always found extra work for us. Their philosophy seemed to be that the devil makes work for idle hands; but as far as I was concerned the devil's work was already being done by the brothers.

Typically the extra work meant prising rocks out of the muddy fields, then carrying them to an adjacent field where we placed them on a growing pile. We usually did this task in single file and clearly some of the rocks were too heavy or slippery for some of the boys. I was struggling to keep hold of my rock and my right leg was stretched behind me when the lad behind me dropped his boulder straight onto my outstretched leg. My involuntary reaction was to drop my own; luckily on to the ground rather than the lad in front.

The pain from the injury almost caused me to pass out; everyone could see the blood coursing down my leg.

The flesh behind my knee had been ripped apart but there didn't appear to be anything broken.

Titch had come running over when he heard my scream and as soon as he had seen what had happened he really laid into the lad who had dropped the stone. Battering him to the ground he was still kicking him as he lay in the mud crying for his mother.

For me and my injury there was no concern at all; he seemed more interested in the opportunity to lay about one of the boys.

Whilst this was going on one of the older boys took off his braces and fastened them tightly around my thigh as one would with a tourniquet. "This might stop the bleeding," he said to me.

The brother on seeing this small act of compassion then turned his attention on my benefactor.

He couldn't get this lad to fall to the ground and the child just stood there and took the beating being administered. His failure to beat the lad to the ground led to the brother's loss of face and his authority took as big a bashing. From that day on two brothers tended their youthful charges. I for my part was allowed to go to the doctor's surgery and was half carried there by two boys delegated to accompany me. To this day I still have the scar despite the best attentions of the school's doctor. I was soon fit enough to be back at work in the milking sheds and carrying out the other farm duties.

Because I was going to be limping for some time Titch dreamed up a job that would keep me in the one place. Handing me a sledgehammer he directed me to two huge granite blocks measuring perhaps ten feet by four.

"I want you to smash these into small pieces," he said with a smirk. He thought the rocks were bigger than me. Again he was proved wrong. This twelve-year old skinny kid called on strength beyond his years and for weeks the sledgehammer rose and fell monotonously.

The chippings would fly everywhere and my bare legs became pockmarked with the constant barrage of sharp granite pieces. Again, the scars stayed with me for life as did the scars on my heart. Often these wounds would bleed a little too profusely at which time the lady doctor would rub some embrocation on my legs.

I might easily have been a chain gang prisoner and yet I was still a child. Perhaps they were harsher on a child because a youngster was denied the strength and spirit to retaliate. If it wasn't me being randomly picked upon and beaten then it was another of the school's kids.

This was for us normal routine. There was no reason for us to believe it was different at any other such establishment. None of us had anything to compare it with and we accepted our lot with bad grace but without a thought that the excesses being carried out would one day horrify the world.

When not fucking around carrying or breaking rocks throughout the winter we were set to work hauling on ropes to remove trees. This was accomplished by tying the rope to the tree about two thirds of the way up. Having done this we would set about undermining its roots with our shovels, spades and picks. We worked hard until each tree's hold on the earth was weakened enough for us to haul it down. A tree's roots are almost as extensive as are its branches. Not surprisingly it could take days just to remove one tree. When the tree was weakened, Titch would line us up very much as depicted in etchings of slaves at work on the pyramids.

Then we in unison would tug steadily on the rope whilst the Christian Brother, stick flailing, would run up and down the line whacking us with the bamboo stick screeching: "Pull, Pull, and Pull!"

This procedure could go on for hours with the tree as set on holding on to the earth as we were set on removing it.

We daren't give up; if we did so then Titch would work himself into a frenzy in the belief that harder strikes and louder screams would achieve what muscle power couldn't.

To this day I have no idea why the farm's tractors were not used to dislodge the trees. But you can't whip and scream at a tractor. We often wished we were as unfeeling.

After each tree had finally been wrenched from the ground we would set about cutting it into pieces using cross-saws. The logs would then be carried up to the brothers' quarters.

All of this took up time and again it seemed the brothers were determined to keep us working even when there was no real work to be done.

The industrial school was self-sufficient. Its livestock included cattle, pigs, chickens, and sheep. There was no shortage of fish and of course an abundance of wheat, vegetables and corn. The turf needed for the fires was cut from our own bogs; we were even rented out to local farmers at hay and turf cutting time. Everything on the industrial school's lands was fashioned into the perfect slave plantation. To these local farms I was sent out many a time and always had with us a packed lunch that included an urn of weak tea that would turn to stodge after hours of lying in the urn's.

I refuse to believe the local population were unaware of the mistreatment and it was apparent that we were considered to be an economic asset to the locality. One can only suppose our misdemeanors, which accounted for some but not all of us, removed us from presumption of kindliness or compassion. The cattle were treated far better than we were. In the eyes of the pious villagers we were all criminals and thoroughly deserved the ill treatment.

Chapter 6

One afternoon I was back from the farm and in the dormitory changing my clothes when Brother Chinney came out of his room. "What are you doing here boy?" he asked.

"I'm getting changed into some dry clothes."

"Come down to my room when you're changed."

I had no idea what he might want of me as having changed I made my way to his room. What does he want I wondered? I went to his room to see a single bed on the right; a wardrobe and dressing table. There was a large window facing out on to the courtyard below. There was a spy-hole carved into the wall and it was clear the brother could see through the spy-hole whilst lying on his bed and as I entered I found him lying on his back on his bed on top of the bedding.

Strangely, his hands were beneath his cassock as he lay there.

"Come; sit on the bed," he said.

I thought to myself, no fucking way. "I am okay here," I said: "What do you want?"

"It's only a little chat I want with you." He said

From the way he was stretched out on the bed I could see why he was called Chinney. His chin was unnaturally long and pointed too. I could see his hands moving briskly under his cassock.

"Do you masturbate?" he asked.

Masturbate? What the fuck is that I thought to myself. In fact I was thinking fast and already trying to figure out an escape strategy. Not wishing to appear stupid I told him I did so sometimes.

"Oh," he said thoughtfully. "And when you come do you do it a second time?"

I am now thinking what the hell is this nutter talking about. "Yes, sometimes three times," I reply thinking this might be the answer he is looking for. In the meantime I can't help but notice his hand movements under the cassock are speeding up and he has a silly lopsided grin on his face.

"Sit beside me, boy; sit beside me now."

I am twelve-years old for goodness sake and by this time I am totally confused and getting really worried. Turning on my heel I blurted out that I had to be off and I then legged it through the door. I glance over my shoulder and can see him chasing after me with what appears to be a truncheon tenting his priestly smock. My feet are flying as I run the length of the dormitory. There's no way I am sitting by that fucker I am thinking to myself as I take to me heels. Fleeing down the stairway I fled across the yard and up the steps. Seeing no one about I carry on running by the carpentry and tailoring rooms on my right hand side and without any pre-thought realise I am escaping the industrial school.

Dressed only in short trousers, boots, a shirt, jersey and short jacket I head up through the gates and take a right turn along the lane in the direction of the church. There is a building on my left and a gate leading into one of the fields where we did our rock carrying. Over the gate I go with bitter memories of my having hurt my leg there as I plan my way around the mountain's side to see if I can find a main road and hoping that I will be heading in the right direction.

I kept on running, gasping for breath and occasionally dropping to a fast walk. I wasn't going as far or as fast as I should, given the mud of the watery bog and the gorse which scratched my legs.

It was soon starting to get dark but I could still see the mountain's shape behind me on my right hand side as it seemed to stretch forever.

Soon I came across a river and had to take a time consuming detour to get across it. By this time I was starving and frozen to the marrow.

It was no place to stop; I had to keep going and my thoughts focused on finding a house or barn where I might find shelter. Knowing St. Patrick had banished all the snakes from Ireland seemed to take away the fear of been bitten by one in the long grass and by the time the moon rose I could see a little more clearly. In fact I was impressed at how well I could see in the dark; all the carrots my ma had given me for dinner no doubt.

After some time I could see a hedge and a brick wall and set my feet towards it and in doing so found I was in luck; I was now on a road that seemed to stretch out in front of me in the distance. It would make the going much easier and enable me to cover greater distances. The thought gave me renewed energy and with feet pounding away I ran with foggy breaths issuing from my mouth as I sucked in air to keep me going. I had covered less than half a mile when I heard the voice:

"Stop, you little bugger."

Fuck. Unable to see where the voice came from I think to myself: "It is a banshee or a ghost."

By this time I am in the middle of the road and I am going like the clappers of hell flat out. You will never catch me I am thinking to myself as my small feet pounded the metalled road. At that point the big copper comes leaping out of the hedge ahead of me and I run straight into his arms. As I do so I am kicking and screaming, my arms and legs flailing.

"Calm down, boyo; calm down." He is saying as he holds me in his grasp. "It is okay. You're safe and I will take care of you shush, shush calm down now."

As though to further reassure me he offers me a toffee: "Now just stand there and don't think of doing any more running. Retrieving a big torch from his tunic he switches the beam on and points it to the sky. I can see its beam reaching as high as the low clouds as he seems to twist and turn it to make some type of signal. "Just be good," he says. "We'll soon have you home, and you will be warm and dry in no time."

After about ten to fifteen minutes I could hear a car approaching and as soon as it gets near I can see it is the big estate car that first took me to the school by the brother. By now I am so exhausted and distraught I collapse into the car's backseat as the copper joins me.

It would seem he was just dropped off on the road on the off chance he might see me as they would know the best vantage points to hide in.

"You little bastard," grimaces Friar Tuck from the driver's seat: ""You have had everyone up this night with no one getting any sleep and boyo you will pay dearly for that."

Dropping the policeman off at the Garda station which is just before the industrial school we carried on up to the school from where I am dragged from the car and more or less kicked across the yard and up the stairs into the shower room, I was allowed shower following which I was put to bed. I was starving; no surprise about that but what did surprise me was that I hadn't received the beating I had been expecting. Little did I know what punishment was going to be mine for there was no precedence to what I had done; no one had ever just run off on an escape before like that.

On the following morning, after church and upon our return to the yard, I heard Chinney calling me over. Right away I knew I didn't like the mad look on his face.

And how he was looking at me with his eyes bulging out of their sockets, he looked demented to say the least.

"Run! Run!" he screamed at me over and over again. I had no idea what he meant. "Run, you little bastard; run, run, run."

Holding up his cassock with both arms he started to kick my arse as I began to run around the yard: "Every time you enter the yard you run, you hear me? You run, you little bastard."

"You will run till you drop and then you will get up and run again" Do you hear me?

And so from that moment on each time I entered the yard I was never allowed to stand nor sit; I had to run all the time when in the yard. This meant there were days when I might have to run for several hours but that weren't the end of it. Saturday night was cinema night, a time when we could all gather in the hall to watch a movie. We boys always sat on one side of the hall, the villagers on the other. As I believe that our hall was the only source of Cinema in the area for the local people.

On the first Saturday after my unsuccessful escape, before the villagers arrived, I was taken up onto the stage. There I had my trousers tugged down and with my arse facing the crowd of lads who were assembled for the film I was made to touch my toes. I was then beaten, receiving a ferocious of amount strokes given by Chinney using his special leather. After about four lashes my arse was on fire. All I could hear was his gasping and grunting as he laid into me with his leather. I was then taken to the rear of the hall where the projection room was situated and made to face the wall. The pain was such that my knees threatened to buckle and my sobs were wrenching my body apart.

I could only think that relief from the pain could only come through death. Eerily, the movie commenced after the villagers arrived and settled themselves in. They each passed me by but not a single one of them remarked on my plight.

They placidly sat and watched the film from where they could plainly see and hear a child sobbing his heart out; they were unmoved. I am sure the movie moved them more.

Neither then nor now was I looking for forgiveness for my attempted escape; I just thought it remarkable that there were so many who knew of such terrible abuses but never uttered a word. The running rule in the yard carried on for three months and Chinney, when on duty took pleasure in helping me around by taking flying kicks at my arse. I also faced the wall in the cinema for the same three months.

What I had been subjected to was not a deterrent but hatred was to grow within me for all the brothers. I was more than ever determined they would never get the better of me no matter what they did to me. It wasn't revenge, it was justice; a justice that would put rights the wrongs of yesterday and ensure their never being repeated.

Some kids went home for Christmas but I never did. Throughout the season of goodwill in Letterfrack the beatings and a myriad of other abuses continued as normal. One winter's evening we boys were in the school's hall playing table tennis; each game's winner getting the chance to stay at the table until he was beaten. I had become very good at this game and had a fast and mean serve. As a consequence I hogged the tables.

One of the Christian Brothers nicknamed Tea; a lanky brother who wore spectacles, would make me give up a table even when I was winning. One night in particular he started screaming at me for winning as often as I did. Taking hold of my arms he dragged me down the hall where there was a turf box measuring I suppose six feet by two. Its contents were used to hold the blocks of turf if the braziers were lit. This night the box was about half full.

Shoving me into the box on top of the turf he then ordered some of the other lads to sit on its lid and bang like hell on it. Rarely have I been so frightened; I was convinced I would be smothered and to this day I am unable to stand anything covering my face. This torture was kept up for what I was told was thirty minutes but it seemed longer. This was because my crime was being good at table tennis and so I made the decision not to be good at anything in the future. All it did was provoke jealousy and that brought cruel penalties.

Christmas came and went and was notable only by my having received some money and a card of course, from my ma and da, brother and sisters. They sent money whenever they had a little to spare and never missed a card when it was my birthday or Christmas. The money could be spent at the sweet shop; there was a good choice of sweets, crisps and mineral drinks.

The winter was cold but the turf still had to be cut in blocks from the bogs.

Off we would go, the small column of hapless waifs and strays, walking two abreast through the farm and up the hill to the bogs. Sometimes I was given the job of cutting, which was easier than was picking and stacking.

I would deftly slice into the sod before throwing the turf chunk on to the bank. The other kids would then carry them using their bare hands to deposit them on little stacks. There were snappy cold breezes up there; perfect for drying them out. One can only picture the grey images of underfed freezing kids, carrying frozen sod-blocks in their bare hands. Some would literally cry out, such was the pain of their chapped raw hands but brother Titch showed no concern towards any of them. He would just keep bellowing at us; urging us to work faster telling us the faster we worked the warmer we would become.

It was a vicious circle; if you had it good as a cutter in the morning you paid the price when during the afternoon you were picking the sods up and carrying them to the stacks. You just gritted your teeth and got on with it, all the time crying inside. At this stage of my life I had finally figured out that prayers went unheard. Those responsible for our religion and welfare were heartless and often sadistic. I began to identify God as being equally unfeeling.

Often several of us were selected to go outside to work on other people's bogs. It was on one such occasion I set out with about ten other boys. Where we were heading wasn't too far away; about a mile in the direction of Kylemore Abbey. Arriving about 8.30am it was to the best of my recollection a miserable bitterly cold day and we were to be the stackers; ferrying blocks of frozen turf cut by the locals.

We had been hard at it for about two hours when one of the smaller kids lost his footing, slipped off the bank and into the sodden bog. It was like a cess pit and if it was as cold in the dry air the frozen state of the water hardly bears thinking about. Titch looked on at the spectacle, quite unmoved as locals ran to the child's aid. One of them jumped in and immediately began to sink as we watched the terrifying drama.

Two of the locals took off their jackets and using them, and one of the staffs, they were able to pull both boy and man from the bog. Luckily they were both unharmed apart from being soaked through and so frozen their teeth were chattering and they were shivering uncontrollably. The kid was as white as a ghost and not surprisingly was in shock. For once we were not left out into the cold but taken back to the school immediately so the group's boys could be showered and given dry clothes.

What would have been the final outcome if the kid had slipped into the mire on our own school bog, as Titch would not have come to his aid and the consequences I could not think about.

Chapter 7

It had since been decided I should go back to working on the farm, milking cows and doing the other farm chores. These jobs I didn't mind. Certainly I had to rise at first light but there aren't many brothers involved in this work.

The local man in charge of the farm is a large pipe-smoking fat man who wears a hat most of the time. He normally dresses in a brown jacket and tucks his grey slacks into his wellie boots. It's his son who is mostly present in the mornings; this is the dapper one who loves to whack his stick on the side of his wellies.

Some time the milking can be great fun but not when the cow kicks the bucket. One that I am milking seems to have sores on her teats and can get agitated when being milked. In one week she had kicked the bucket three times. This meant I had to be punished. On two nights I went to bed hungry, my supper having been denied.

We would kneel at our bedsides while Chinney would recite a decade of the rosary.

Then we would recite out loud "Now I lay me down to sleep I pray to God my Sole to keep. If I die before I wake I pray to God my sole to take.

Pray. Pray. And more Praying, I wish someone would pray for me this night as I am starving, cold and so lonely.

But why do they pray these brothers? Why do what they do and then they pray? I cannot understand it; it makes no sense to me.

I know I am afraid of heights but I am even more afraid of starving to death so on the second night, at about four in the morning, I went to the washroom and slid the window up.

I was then able to get out of the window and shin down the building's drainpipe to reach the ground floor.

Creeping silently along the outside wall I finally reached a window set in the wall beside the door leading to the dining room. Climbing up I managed to open this window and to then clamber through it before venturing across the dark and deserted dining room: There was a bread press from which I took a loaf. Creeping back the way I had come, taking care to close the window behind me, I worked my way up the drainpipe again and into my bed where I sent half of it down my neck. Hardly surprisingly the bout of hiccups stayed with me for most of the day but I was at least full and it would be filled the next night when the other half would follow the first.

Besides nourishing my belly I had learned that I could get out of the dorm without being seen; and Brother Chinney did indeed sleep and couldn't hear everything.

On the farm there were many hogs and sows; these were kept in small buildings opposite the cowsheds where the milking was done. There was one morning when for some reason I arrived earlier than usual and thought I had the place to my own.

I was in the cowshed going about my work when I heard one of the pigs squealing in a way I hadn't before heard.

Curious, I peered through the window to see what was causing the strange noises. My jaw dropped as I watched the farmer's son exiting the big sow's shed. Running, he jumped over the wall to land in the yard, nearly stumbling as he did so and I could clearly see his Mickey [penis] hanging out of his trousers as he fumbled with the front of his trousers. As he recovered his composure he was staring about him and looking guilty as hell before walking off to the back of the yard. What was all that about I found myself wondering?

It was much later in life that the penny dropped about what he had being doing in the shed with the sow. And it was us who were supposed to be bad kids?

One day the head farmer told me the big sow was going to have bohniefs [piglets] and suggested I stay to help him deliver them. We had her in a separate pen to the normal sty and she was lying on a bet of straw. We settled ourselves down in there from late afternoon. The farmer had everything prepared for what could be a long wait and there were as many cups of tea as we wanted. It was a long wait for it was 5am the following day before she started to give birth.

My God, the piglets just kept slipping out of the mother. The farmer would cut the cord as each emerged, dab a little iodine on the piglet's tummy and then place each youngster in a straw-filled box. It was a sight to see when the twelve of them were finally nesting in there. All little pink things and with all their squealing it was bedlam.

"Now, boy," he says to me: "You have to take their teeth out so they won't bite their mother when she is suckling."

Producing a pair of pliers he methodically began to pull the teeth one by one. As he did so he put each of the tiny mites to their mother's teats so they could feed. He told me it had been a grand night and says: "That's more money for the brothers' coffers." At that time I never quite understood what he meant by that.

By the time the birthing was finished it was gone 8am and I was given permission to go to my bed in the dorm. Apart from a couple of kids who were sick I had the place to myself. That was until mid-afternoon when Chinney joined me in the washroom as I was freshening up.

"What are you doing here?" he asks me.

I told him about the pig and piglets at which point he came close to me and taking my wrist he pushed my arm up my back, like you hold a partner when dancing, before pulling me on to his knee. Putting his face very close to mine it seemed that he intended to kiss me. Fuck this, I thought to myself.

"You come any closer to me and I will bite your fucking nose off," I warned him. The words were hardly out of my mouth when he angrily threw me across the washroom floor. I came to a stop under the sink to find my head had hit something and I was bleeding badly from the cut.

"You little bastard," he screamed: "I will finish you here; I will finish you for good, you little bastard."

I was crying, terrified and trying to hold my injured head; my hands were covered in blood and the pain was making me feel sick. It was then that one of the ailing boys that was in the dorm in bed came into the washroom. He must have heard the commotion. Chinney just glared at me and stomped out of the room with his mad eyes bulging out of their sockets.

Grabbing a towel I tried to stem the blood before going down the stairs where I found Friar Tuck standing at the sweet shop. He took one look at me and then it was off to the doctor for her to patch me up. The sweet shop is very close to and just below the washroom so the brother manning it must have heard what had gone on and drawn his own conclusions. He didn't mention anything. The brother's always looked after their own.

Four stitches were needed to pull the torn scalp together. My fear of Chinney was now greater than ever and I was worried about what was going to happen next. I would have to be on my guard at all times as there was no one to turn to for help or no one to tell of my fears. A lot of the lads in Letterfrack were orphans or placed there for the most trivial of matters; often temporary problems at home.

Often they were sent there because their father and mother had split and were no longer living together.

Others were there for missing school and others were petty thieves; sent to keep the company of career thieves and those who were simply born bad. It was a one size fits all societal a refuse dump for the unfortunates and miscreants. Out of sight and out of mind; certainly mindless.

The thinking behind the setting up of industrial schools is beyond my comprehension, unless there were ulterior motive; economic or otherwise. The environment could hardly have benefited potentially good and aspiring youngsters. Letterfrack and other industrial schools like them were exemplary only as a means of educating all youngsters, at the crack of a whip or an oath, to be influenced and educated by society's low-life. Their period of detention would leave them ideally suited to despising the society that had nurtured them, and to react accordingly throughout the rest of their lives.

These industrial schools were universities of infamy that corrupted both supervisors and their hapless detainees. Each was a bloodstain of the Republic's escutcheon.

Fights between boys were a daily occurrence and the weaker children, when not beaten or abused by the brothers were battered senseless and ill-treated by the bigger and older boys. Such aggression was channeled or rather turned into entertainment by Br. Tea who decided he would hold a boxing match in the hall. Instructing us to fashion a boxing ring or sorts from four benches he produced a couple of pair of boxing gloves. Then, with careful deliberation he lines us up along the wall, decided on one of the taller lads and handing him the gloves he ordered him into the ring.

Pulling me out from the row and handing me a pair of gloves he said: "There you go boyo. Let's all have a good laugh will we he said?" With a big grin on his face.

Climbing over one of the benches and into the makeshift arena I am thinking; fuck; I am dead. This moron is going to kill me.

Reasoning that the best form of defense was to attack I shot out of my corner towards my opponent and landed a straight right to his chin. Startled by the speed and ferocity of the assault the taller lad lost his footing and landed on his back. I am not sure who was the most surprised; him or me. By Jesus, thought I. I can do for him.

I was sadly mistaken if I thought Br Tea would be impressed. Stumped at my unexpected triumph he gave my adversary all the time he needed to recover his wits and his confidence. The boy then came at me flailing but ducking under his swinging arms I struck out and smacked him good and proper on the back of his head as he ducked. Again he crumpled to his knees. What was happening gave weight to the maxim: It isn't the size of the dog in the fight; it's the size of the fight in the dog.

Even so I was still frightened out of my wits and all I could think of was that I had to avoid being hit by him because if one of his roundhouses connected he would lay me out. Undeterred by my effectiveness he bounced to his feet and was soon all over me, raining punches and hoping one of them would decide the matter once and for all. From somewhere I couldn't fathom I was keeping up my strength and spirit and didn't fall to any of his punches. Again I struck out and this time caught him on the chin; again he fell to his knees.

At this point Br Tea decided enough was enough and the fight should end there and now. Taking the other lad's arm and holding it erect he declared him the winner. I had dropped him three times; he hadn't put me down once but he was declared the victor. At least I had learned that strength isn't related to size and that was a valuable lesson that would sustain me through life.

Br Tea lost interest in boxing having backed a loser and whatever his actions the rest of the boys knew him to be a cheat, even the beaten boy knew that. The brother had lost credibility and been exposed as a cheat; worse; a cheat who loses. Winters are very cruel on Ireland's western Atlantic coast but there was no allowance made for the harsh weather; we dressed more or less as we did in summer regardless of season. We were issued with heavier socks, a vest and a pullover but still wore shorts and so our legs were often literally blue with the cold. The only fire place was the one in the hall. It wasn't very big so just a few lads were able to gather around it. If you were small then you had very little chance of drawing any heat.

Fights among the lads continued to be a daily occurrence; it was the one anti-social activity that was tolerated by the cruel brothers. One day, outside the church a bigger kid was trashing a much younger and smaller one when he lost his footing. Immediately seizing his advantage the younger kid immediately got on top and straddled the bigger boy's chest. He then began to repeatedly head-butt his tormentor, lunging his forehead into the older lad's face until there was blood everywhere.

The younger boy's rage had given him a maniacal fury and his adversary was unconscious by the time the maddened youngster was dragged clear. That younger boy was to later become one of Ireland's most notorious gangland criminals. No doubt such tenure was honed by his experiences at Letterfrack.

Brutality and fear was never far distant. It was a Saturday evening when I accidentally bumped into a bigger kid who was carrying a lot of weight. Despite my protestations that it was an accident he wasn't too pleased and probably saw opportunity for channeling his aggression. I was challenged to a fight in the lower washroom toilets the following morning.

All that night I tossed and turned whilst sleep evaded me; I was convinced I was going to be thoroughly trashed the following morning. Clap! Clap! Clap! Chinney is up to his early morning wake-up routine and we all hear him barking. It is now back to reality for me and I face a fight with a bully whom I have no chance of beating. I had little alternative but to head towards the washrooms where it is freezing cold and the winter's mist hangs over the outside yard like a wet blanket.

Fatty is there waiting for me: I had hardly walked through the door when the blow struck me on the back of my head. I fell to the floor from its force, thinking to myself; I am fucked here.

It was then I remembered that bigger is not necessarily stronger; I remembered also the tables being turned when the smaller of the two boys got the upper hand in the churchyard scrap.

Leaping to my feet with the agility of a cat I ran straight at the fat bully and we trade blows. Clearly there isn't going to be a winner when neither is prepared to give ground.

The blows traded between us became fewer and soon, gasping for breath, we paused as we eyed each other up and down. It was he who broke the stalemate.

"Quit?"

"Quit!"

We shook hands on it as he says to me; "You're some goer for a little fucker" before heading towards the stairs whilst hoping we had not been missed and our disheveled state wouldn't be noticeable.

The rest of the kids were wondering which of us had won and their jaws dropped; you could have cut the silence with a knife as we both walked in as friends. Chinney seemed unaware of the fracas, which was a relief.

He was too absorbed in one of the school's newer kids and I am thinking to myself, Lord, help him.

The longest road is the one that leads nowhere I was thinking; and out here in one of the most depopulated areas of western Ireland in the nineteen sixties truly is best called nowhere. I persevered and took each day as it came; did any child ever pay a higher price for being too trusting in his friends and such a minor infraction as entering a social club for pennies? I felt sometime the wretchedness would never end.

We are into February and there's little of the daylight as dawn seems to go straight into dusk and those longest nights are unending. I have got my arm caught up in a thorn bush, one of which has become bedded in my skin bringing with it signs of infection. Taken to the doctor I learn that a poultice is to be applied. Boiling bread in a pot she applies the still heat-sizzling pasta to my arm. Fucking hell the searing pain was nigh unbearable. How can this be helping I ask myself: She is worse than the fucking brothers.

"Keep this on," she says as she wraps a bandage around it. Come and see me tomorrow."

It is small compensation that I get the rest of the day off. I would rather have worked the farm. So there I am, wandering around the yard aimlessly when Chinney spots me. Calling me over he asks me what I am doing there and I explained to him what happened.

"Go up to the dormitory," he says: "I will be up there shortly."

When I got to the dormitory I found it unusually empty; there's invariably at least one ailing child in bed.

Walking the hall's length to where the brothers' quarters are I stand outside Chinney's room door. Br. Tea's room is on the opposite side of the corridor.

It is while I am standing there that I notice for the first time there are windows over each of the doors and both are open.

Although they are quite small I am convinced I could get through either of them. I keep this revelation to myself; it might have some future use.

After a while Chinney appears, takes out a bunch of keys from his cassock; inserts a key into the door's lock and pushes it open.

"In you go, lad."

Here we go again. This fucker just doesn't give up I think as he lies on his bed and on this occasion on his side facing me. He lights a cigarette and draws on it as he coolly looks me up and down. The cigarettes are Sweet Afton in their familiar yellow packet. Smiling he takes another drag and then asks me if I would like one. To be honest I could kill for one but smelling a rat I told him I would not.

"What? You don't smoke? Little rats from Dublin start at about seven years old. Take one," he adds as he offers the opened packet. "I am just being friendly."

"No thanks; I don't smoke."

"I see you are back on the farm. How are you getting on there?"

"I like it fine," I tell him. "I love the openness of it all and I am learning lots of things."

"Good, good, It is what you are here for," he says still smiling as he presses the cigarette's butt into the ashtray that is already brimming with cigarette ends. "Have you been masturbating recently?"

"No!"

God, I think to myself; not again?

Chinney says looking at me thoughtfully. "Good: You know, if you ever got married your future wife will know you have been masturbating: She will know just by looking at your Mickey [penis]. Would you like me to look at your Mickey [penis] so I can tell you if she is going to know?"

"No, I don't think so," I answered defiantly.

"You are never going to learn are you?"

"Yes, I am learning," I retorted. "I am learning not to come up to your room on my own ever again." I paused and then added: "Brother. I do not like this and I am very afraid of what is happening.

Can I please go now and I will not say anything to anyone? I have not spoken a word about the other times so please, please, can I go now?"

"You will stay till I tell you to go," he tells me and with that he places his right hand under his cassock and started fiddling around as if trying to locate something. I am rooted to the spot and afraid I will get a battering or worse. As my mind races he starts moving his hand up and down but keeps it under his cassock. Again he is wearing that stupid lopsided grin on his leering face. His chin is protruding and the effect is exaggerated as he hasn't yet shaved. With his black hair he looks as evil as Satan himself.

"Come boy, come closer to me," he murmurs whilst his hands continue doing ninety to the dozen under his cassock.

"I am okay here, sir."

"Come, boy. Lie with me here."

It is getting time to leg it again but I am conscious of the bitterly cold weather out there; perishing cold and unprotected one wouldn't last long on the windswept moors of the Atlantic facing county. He then lets out a long sigh and both he and his hand relax as he closes his eyes whilst I wonder what next?

His eyes opened for several moments and I can't help but notice how piercing blue they are and they shine brightly. "Go now, boy; and not a word to anyone. Do you hear me? Not a word!"

Leaving the room there's a strong sense of relief that he hasn't at least physically abused me but I can't help wondering how long my luck can hold. How long before he goes too far and rapes me; with my skinny frame I would be no match for his physical strength.

As I descend the stairs in silence I notice the sweet shop door is open and so I dawdle a bit and listen carefully. After several minutes Friar Tuck emerges and walking into the yard lights a cigarette. I notice he has left the shop door open. Sneaking inside I grab the first thing I can lay my hands on; bars of chocolate.

Withdrawing quietly and moving as quietly as I could I made my way down the corridor, past the doctor's surgery and then to the downstairs jacks. As soon as I close the cubicle door behind me I wolf down the contents of the wrappers. Such is the mess around my mouth I put my head under the tap to wash away the evidence.

I have learned a couple of things today; one is the windows being left open over the brothers' room doors, two that Friar Tuck seems to leave the shop door open every other afternoon, especially when he goes out to the yard for a smoke.

A plan is formulating in my mind about my next escape. It won't be as foolhardy as the previous unplanned flight. Next time I will be prepared.

Staying here will only be worse for me now I am aware what Chinney and the kitchen cook are up to with the younger kids. But who will believe me?

Next morning I go to the doctor to have the poultice removed. As she pulls it off out comes this long string of gunk, loads of it.

"You will be fine now," she says; "We extracted the poison just in time so lucky for you. You could have lost the power of your right arm so you have got to be more careful in future she tells me.

Even after a long day in the fields or bog it is sometimes difficult to get off to sleep. I often find myself drifting into dreams or should I say thoughts of past times that already growing more distant. Thinking of the past stops it all disappearing and I have to stay connected with my past, my ma and da, brother, sisters and of course Dublin. I can still remember making my holy communion in Ringsend Church. This is where my Ma hails from and if you were from Ringsend you were called a Raytowner. This expression derived from the Stingray; a lovely fish to eat and I find it as palatable today as I did then.

Getting ready for your Holy Communion was a big occasion. You used to go to confession on a regular basis but you could not take communion at mass because you had not made it as yet. I remember one day there were a lot of boys in the queue for the confession box as we had all come from school to do a trial run.

"Bless me father. I have sinned," one would say.

He would then ask you to list your sins but what sins does a seven year old have? I told lies twice, father: I stole a biscuit from my sister and suchlike. But they always asked "did you have any bad thoughts or deeds? At seven I don't think so.

On the day of my Holy Communion there were about three kids in front of me when I started to feel like I wanted to piss! Shit will they ever hurry up, what's keeping them in there?

By this stage I so wanted a pee that I was nearly doubled up with bladder cramps. Into the confession box I trot and pulling out my Mickey I could almost hear the hissing as in a vain attempt to minimize a puddle I spray the booth. By the time the priest pulled the panel back and gave me his blessing I was kneeling in my own puddle of urine.

"Bless me, my father; I have sinned."

"Yes, my son. And do tell me what those sins are."

"I am kneeling in a pool of piss in here."

"You're what?" he bellows

"Kneeling in piss, father. Someone has pissed in your box."

The small door promptly opened as he exited the confessional box and coming around to where I am kneeling he reaches in and drags me out. "Boy! Why have you done this?"

"No, no," I tell him earnestly."

I knew the kid who had gone before me was well out of sight and justice by now. By this time a small crowd of older people begun to gather and I hear a voice saying: "Oh, the poor lad: He has gone and wet his self"

The priest was looking for the teacher; he just wanted me off his hands but it wasn't so easy for me. I had started to cry as my pants bore silent witness to my sin.

My front is wet and the teacher cannot but see that I was the culprit. Why don't they put toilets in churches? Maybe priests don't piss or shite.

It wasn't long before a cleaning lady approached with her bucket and mop. Dabbing me dry she mopped out the confessional box too. There had been a similar occasion at Letterfrack. I had woken very early and had no idea of the time but I could feel the front of my nightshirt was sopping warm wet.

The mattress too was moist and I knew right then I had pissed my own bed. I couldn't be certain it wasn't a dream but I was cute enough to do whatever was necessary to avoid Chinney knowing of my fall from grace.

Silently creeping to the bathroom I rang out the nightshirt. Then, returning to the dormitory I quietly stripped the sheets from the bed and exchanged them for dry ones from the cupboard. Climbing back into bed I waited for the brother's handclapping, which I knew was imminent. All had gone well; he never did find out. I relished my escape because I could well imagine the joy of Chinney had he discovered I had pissed the bed. Making the most of it the punishment would have included me running around the yard, holding the sheeting up with the air flowing behind me. This was a favorite form of chastisement but it didn't have the desired effect; all it did was humiliate and exhaust the unfortunate bed wetter. One can only wonder at the mentality of the people who dreamed such punishments up. One could suppose them to be far greater sinners than were we 'inmates.'

It might be presumed some of the Christian Brothers were kindly and those who were not were in the minority; the difficulty was in identifying them. As a body they kept themselves to themselves and they stuck together in a form of herd self-protectionism. All had good reason for not drawing attention to them selves. It was all for one and one for all.

Today we are sowing spuds and each of us are on bare knees and constantly prodding a small stick into the soil in the ploughed furrows. Dropping the seeds in we then pulled the soft earth over them; pat to firm and move on to the next seedlings. Everything was done by hand; everything except the ploughing but I swear before God that if they could find a way to harness a child to a plough they would have done so; even a team of us.

We could at least talk between ourselves, even banter when we were working the fields. I hadn't made friends as such but there were a few boys I chatted to. The lad working with me today was a fellow Dubliner. He was a tall lad from the district of Drimminagh who looked a lot older than his fourteen years.

He was chatting away about some old person who lived near him at home. She was by his account a woman who, despite having six children, was perfectly gorgeous. So much so, he said, you could eat chips out of her knickers. Yes, even without the salt and vinegar. He wouldn't shut up about her, all the time repeating: "She was made for love. You could smell the sex off her."

"Did you ever ride her," I asked him. I had no idea what the expression actually meant but had heard it often said.

"No, not yet," he replied but added that as soon as he was released he would make a play for her. "I can see her now," he added: "Lying with her legs up in the air and me jumping her."

"Jesus," I thought. "Is that how you do it; you jump on her? Maybe that was why they have big diddies, to break our fall? Fuck! I shall like to do that sometime.

"Move along, you bastards; move along or you will never get these rows finished today."

I never heard any more about jumping on women; instead we got thousands of seeds of another kind planted during that balmy spring day. It wasn't in fact a bad day as days go in Connemara. We worked hard until nightfall and then as always, two abreast we wended our way back to Letterfrack Industrial School As we progressed Titch kept on wielding his stick, striking out at the younger kids. He just couldn't help himself; he was programmed to inflict pain on the weakest in society.

Few of us could forget the expression on his face when two of his small charges broke ranks and made off into the adjacent fields. For some reason he was on his own that day and couldn't run after them as had he done so it would have meant abandoning us. All he could do was scream come back, you little bastards, at their retreating forms.

We all started to cheer the small rebels by shouting encouragement to them: "Keep going, lads. Get away!"

As we jumped up and down in excitement, Titch ran up and down the row of boys, lashing out with his cane. Soon the youngsters disappeared into the bogs. Maybe they would get away I thought to myself. Hopefully they would find somewhere they could shelter from the cold night air before the darkness of night really closed in.

Although it was spring the temperatures still plummeted at night to below freezing and the small lakes dotted throughout the bogs were mostly frozen. I was not alone in praying for their safety; not that I was overly keen on God at the moment.

The stick-waving brother moved us all along at a faster pace than we were used to and clearly he couldn't wait to do whatever was necessary to get the young escapees back again. He certainly had some explaining to do and it must have been humiliating to tell the other brothers he had lost two of his charges.

Our yard had a buzz about it and by this time the entire school knew of the escape. Bets were being taken as to the length of time they would remain free. As a former absconder myself I knew what they would be up against and was under no illusions as to their chances of beating the system.

After a little time we were quietened down by the brothers whilst in the distance we could hear cars scouring the lanes; others were coming up the gravel driveways leading to the school itself.

Ushered into the dining hall it was difficult to ignore the buzz of excitement and by 5.30pm we were back in the yard. By now it was fully dark and extremely cold, which conjured up thoughts of the distressing situation the two boys' might now find themselves in. It was possible to die through exposure in the bogs on a cold night when without shelter and especially if wet. We stood around in groups, wondering what had become of the two youngsters, debating whether they would survive the night.

Normally at this time we would be directed to the hall, especially with it being so cold. This was never done for our benefit but for the brothers who were not too keen on the cold. Had they been able to leave us unsupervised in the open they would of course have done so.

It must have been a little after seven o'clock when two cars pulled up outside the school. The doors opened and Titch and Mutton Head emerged, the former having a broad beam on his face. Stretching to getter a better view of what was happening we could see Titch pulling the two hapless waifs from the car. The poor mites were filthy dirty from their time in the bog; their hair was disheveled as it might be when they had just awoken. Both of the boys' were weeping copiously.

Marching them towards the carpenters shop Titch stood the two of them up against the wall. He then took up a big water hose and satisfied he had the pair just where he wanted them he turn the jet of water on them. With a smug grin he then began to hose the two lads down. By this time the temperatures had dropped to well below freezing and not surprisingly the two youngsters were screaming and clutching their arms around themselves for vain protection. Standing close and watching the spectacle with interest were about five of the school's brothers and two men from the village. Not a one of them cried out enough. Shameful.

As he hosed the two boy's down Titch was scream "Bastards, bastards! I will kill you even if it kills me, you bastards."

We could only look on, sickened whilst hoping that the boys' would recover from the treatment being meted out to them. The screams of those two small boys were still ringing in our ears as we mournfully went to our beds that awful night. We checked and they were not in the dormitory so we had no idea what had happened to them. It was rumored they had been forced to sleep naked on the floor but that was hearsay. The next morning the two of them were seen running around the yard as we made our way to mass at the local church. Perhaps God was there? They were the first to run since I had gone through the same ordeal; they were being dealt with just as severely. Their ordeal never deterred me from running away again; in fact all it did was convince me I was right to plan my escape from this hellish place.

They were the first to have gone on the run since I had absconded and the Brothers were dealing with them as severely as they had dealt with me.

Chapter 8

If there was anything good to say about routine it was the rarity of landmark events meant time passed quickly. The days quickly became weeks and with the spring and greener grass; the flowers and the leaves turning the green countryside even greener there was the smell of change mixed with hope in the air.

The brothers tended to leave me to my own devises and as I go about my tasks on the farm I feel comfortable in my own company. There was little change to everyday habits but one day we were told it was time to slaughter a pig. We five chosen to be included in the process gathered a little nervously under the arch of the farmyard's gate. As we did so the sow was taken out of her pen pulled by the rope tied to her neck. Guided to her destiny with fate she was pulled into position under a block and tackle.

We boys held her steady while the brother placing the stun gun's muzzle to her forehead pulled the trigger. There was a loud ear shattering bang. The sow began to kick, slumped and went into unconscious shaking and trembling.

The rope around her neck was quickly untied and deftly her rear legs strapped to the block and tackle's harness. At this point we were told to haul and haul we did until the creature was swinging in the cold spring air of the farmyard.

As soon as she was fully aloft the brother placed some buckets under her head before taking a knife and slicing the animal's neck from ear to ear. In a torrent the blood spurted and fell straight into the buckets. This was to be used to make black puddings we were told. After a little while the flow slowed to a trickle.

At this point the brother again took up his knife and expertly placing it at the dead sow's throat ran it down its belly until it was opened to its midriff. As he did so we watched the sow's entrails slop out on to a square of tarpaulin that had been placed to catch them. Without any sign of squeamishness the brother put his hands into the animal's belly up to his armpits and retrieved its entrails; its heart, liver, spleen and suchlike. These organs were placed in a separate bucket.

Water had been boiled ready for our next task. We boys were each handed a knife with the instruction that we shave the carcass of its hair. We were of course very nervous about being involved in this as we were after all still children. City kids were unlikely to have seen a pig, let alone slaughtered one.

We scraped and scraped until the skin was absent of hair and the carcass was left steaming in the morning air. We were at least being taught how to be butchers and farmers. It was better than learning nothing at all.

It was about this time I became increasingly skeptical about religion and questioned whether it being constantly pushed down our throats was the right way of going about convincing us of the sublime faith. I became more and most distant from the commonly held beliefs. I had little choice but to follow these rituals but my inner thoughts were now repelled by this utter crap we were being force fed with.

We were as orchestrated as the farm animals were; a boy farm to be seeded and harvested. It was beyond my comprehension how the brothers and others who abuse kids, often sexually, could take Holy Communion each day. Could it be me who was wrong?

Was there something I had failed to grasp? Perhaps they could sin at will as long as they begged for forgiveness each day; the confessional being the get out of gaol card. Little wonder I was confused but to me my own philosophy.

If you did not sin then you didn't need the protection of the church. This seemed to settle these vexed matters better for me. Accordingly I would just chant the mantras but doing so without giving them any meaning.

Sunday morning mass was the event at which all villagers were present and would find the saintly priest reading out the names of those locals who had made donations to the church. It would go something like this Mr. *   *   * the local *   *   * one shilling and six pence; Mr. *   *   * the local*   *   * one shilling and so on.

It was a great way of embarrassing locals into shelling out as much as they could. I bet God was happy with the results which found their way into the collection tray. It caused me to wonder how he could ever spend all the money collected each day in all churches around the world whilst we were being starved here.

I was further perplexed by the penny required for the black babies' boxes? These were scattered about everywhere; the industrial school included. Surely the great church couldn't give to them that which was collected each day in their churches? But then I was just an undernourished innocent twelve-year old kid and all of this was just a mystery of faith. It seemed the intention was to keep it a mystery. And so proceeded the institutionalising of we youngsters; all those who had gone this way before and all who would follow. It was the perfect partnership; church and state.

We were never allowed into the village on our own but were marched to its outskirts before taking a left then out of the main gate avoiding its main thoroughfare. We always trooped two abreast.

Because of this we never learned much about the village or its small population. We had little idea of its true size, of how it functioned or who made up its key figures.

Although we too were part of the community there was an ambiguity in the relationships; an apartheid of sorts. Certainly many of the villagers passed among us but we never struck up friendships or got to know them or their purpose; their faith or their backgrounds. We were seen as part of the community but apart from it. We were lesser beings; different. There was no attempt to mingle with us or to get to know us at all. We were non-persons; a ghostly column of coming and going; a presence that was virtually invisible. We were the elephant in the room

The local farmer who was also in charge of our farm had two daughters whom we would see from time to time. There were put to work cooking and cleaning in the big house and would come to mass each Sunday and other holy days. They were often seen at the movies on Saturday nights. This caused me some confusion. I had always been taught girls would have boyfriends and Saturday nights would be the one occasion that might be set aside for their boyfriends.

Their isolation was perhaps a reason why so many country girls from counties like ours would eventually try their luck elsewhere; in cities like London or New York.

There surely they would find contentment; work and husbands. I decided I would go to London or New York when I was older. Little did I realise that my internment at Letterfrack would make it difficult to travel. I was now a confirmed criminal.

The preparations for the summer holidays were by now under way. This was a time when some of the lads would learn if they were to be allowed home for a holiday. I dismissed as fanciful my own chances having been labelled an escapee. I was left behind with about forty other kids for the summer. It was no holiday for us; everything carried on with a brutal and tedious normality.

We were taken swimming on some of the more pleasantly warm days; this was at an inlet about a ten minute walk distant. Again we would sally forth in our little two abreast rows. Turning left we would head off in the direction of Cliften. Climbing over a fence we would then walk the short distance to this small rock-covered cove. From there we were allowed to jump or dive into the sea and to enjoy ourselves. We sported playfully and the memories of doing so enriched my life as little else could. There was such joy in experiencing the freedom of the sea; to imagine for golden moments I was as free as a sea mammal.

This was so different to an occasion that confronted me when I was younger. I had been walking along the banks of a Dublin canal when a group of lads had taken hold of me and fully clothed I was thrown into its murky waters. In a negative sense that cruel experience also remained with me; it was the sense of utter and helpless devastation.

I had submerged with my eyes and mouth open and recall seeing fish swimming before emerging thrashing about and spluttering. From the middle of the canal I somehow managed to doggy paddle to the canal banks.

The bullies thought it was a great fun and could hardly contain them selves on seeing my bedraggled state. What they didn't know was I had been born with The Caul. This meant I would never drown so up their arses, the dopey fuckers. I had pulled myself out of the canal and soaking wet had made my miserable way home. I can still visualise the stares I attracted as I wended my way to my home at Railway Terrace.

Ma was furious when she set eyes on me and saw the state I was in. As soon as she realised what had happened her temper softened, thanking the Lord I had been born with a Caul.

A form of skin membrane that sometimes covers a baby's face when born, she had deposited it in a matchbox in the hospital but it had gone missing. She always swore that a nurse had robbed it to sell to a sailor. Cauls were much sought after by sea going people. The important thing to me wasn't in possessing it; it was my knowing I had been born with one, which meant my never having a fear of water. In truth it might not be more than an old wife's tale. Enough to say that swimming in the cove I was as content as might be a seal.

There was one day when using the cove we saw quite clearly a shark's distinctive fin and there was no doubt in our minds as to the menace that might suggest. The brother looking after us told us not to concern ourselves; he said it was a basking shark and common to these waters. We could also see seals enjoying their environment but for us there was nothing quite like leaping or diving off the rocks into those wonderful inrushing waters of the Atlantic Ocean. Alternatively we would be taken for long walks in the countryside, but wherever we were destined it always led through the main gates and a turn left. There must have been a reason for it but it remained a mystery to me.

So perhaps the holidays weren't so bad after all but there is of course no place quite like home, no matter how humble it is: I missed my home, my ma and my brother and sisters desperately. I did receive letters and money from my ma on a regular basis so was always able to buy sweets. The warmer weather brought another bonus; we could play football in the yard.

I wasn't too bad at soccer and so was picked often. It wasn't a sport we could volunteer for; each of the team's squads was selected on merit by one of the brothers. Luckily for me, the brother who usually arranged the games had taken a likening to me and so I got a game each time one was played.

There was one time I recall when I had come very close to scoring but on the point of taking the shot I was roughly bowled over by one of the bigger players. The brother lit up; he was screaming mad and gave the boy a really good kicking before making him stand facing the wall for what was left of the match,

I was also awarded two penalties; the brother explained that the foul was so bad it merited both attempts. I didn't let him down. I scored each time which pulled us ahead by two goals.

Although this brother showed kindness to me he never ever tried to molest me. He was something of a nutter and I was glad to be on his good side. I wouldn't have wanted to receive a beating from him as he was always very severe.

On other days we would go off to the Gaelic field to play Gaelic football but this game held no interest for me. Hurling was another of the school's favorite sports but this again wasn't my kettle of fish. Soccer suited me just fine.

The work allocated during the summer consisted mostly of working in the fields. There we would pick potatoes by hand and carry them in baskets to a trailer and then empty our baskets into it. At such time as it was full the cart would be towed away by the tractor to the storage shed. Once the fields were harvested the farmer's son would use the same tractor to plough the field for whatever crop was intended for the following season.

Throughout the months following a few of us would be taken to the spud shed, There we would get on to our knees and taking each spud check it for quality; the good ones being placed behind us. This was called turning the spud and my strongest impression of this activity was the rancid smell of the storage shed, the darkness too. By the time the day's work was over your hands stunk to high heaven; they were also much blackened.

It often entered my mind that we could catch the potato blight disease that had led to the famine that so ravaged Ireland a century earlier. Luckily we never did so we were not compelled to emigrate. I was far enough from my home as it was. One would think that being so involved in the dirty side of the potato industry would put one off the things for life, but it never did.

There was neither radio nor television at Letterfrack; nor did we ever set eyes on a newspaper so never had the slightest idea of what was going on in the outside world. Our county is extremely remote; as a form of exile it must have suited the Christian Brothers perfectly for they were far from prying eyes. I received letters from home but they were of family matters, all trivial. I did know that I was the only one to bring shame on the family; the only sibling to get into trouble during my younger years. It was thought I was always in turmoil and looking for whatever I could get up to next. Being the eldest I also was the one who witnessed all of the trouble and strife that went on between my ma and da.

I did in truth have two older brothers but they had been born out of wedlock and one I thought was my uncle. I never discovered he was my brother until I was sixteen. The other brother had been taken away by the nuns. He was to spend the first sixteen years of his life as an orphan of the Irish state. He spent all of his childhood years in industrial schools similar to the one I was incarcerated in at Letterfrack. I never did learn why one brother led a very comfortable childhood as a charge on his grandmother whilst the other undoubtedly must have suffered terribly as a consequence of being left to rot in the notorious industrial schools.

But, these matters were beyond not only my understanding but beyond my influence.

Nevertheless, both brothers blamed me for their dysfunctional childhoods and they were unmoved by my protestations that I had not even been born until years after they were. There needed to be blame apportioned; I was the one it was directed at.

Later on in years the older of the two often took advantage of my easy-going nature; arriving without notice on the presumption that I would give him whatever money he needed.

Needless to say we became estranged, which probably saved me much money. The other was equally demanding and must have thought I was his surrogate mother, expecting me to keep and feed him. To some there are advantages to being disadvantaged and they are cute enough to work it out for themselves.

The industrial schools set-up was a barely disguised system to make use of the nation's disadvantaged boys and girls on an industrial scale; a revolving doors method that was in truth nothing other than state-approved indentured slavery. By contrast our troubles under the British might seem minor for pain feels sharper when inflicted by those of one's own kind.

This in a nation of conviction-led Catholics brings no credit at all to the Republic of Ireland. There are few of its troubadours singing about their self-inflicted troubled times. No one was singing The Fields of Letterfrack.

This system to my knowledge was perfectly acceptable to the nation's judiciary; the apparatus of state including the Garda. All were making money from the miseries inflicted upon the nation's orphans. They were not only deprived of their parents; they were deprived of their statehood, their self respect and their good name. Even those like me, placed there for such crimes as petty stealing, had far more stolen from them by those who had no excuse. To my mind they have no god either. Their status in the community was also a carefully contrived illusion.

There is much sentimentality about Ireland and it is universally regarded with affection; the birthplace of great writers, poets, playwrights; of men of understanding and literature. It seems not to have occurred to anyone to ask why it is the one European country that leads the rest in emigration. In Ireland there is apartheid with a difference; it is less well defined than skin color but it is as prevalent and the scars are as great.

Ireland has been and still is a divided country firmly in the hands of ruling elite that abuses its power as do many Third World countries. It cultivates its carefully manicured image which is out of kilter with reality. Ireland will never share the comparatively prosperous contentment of its fellow European nations and their peoples as long as its affairs are controlled by a self-serving incompetent few whose positions are based not on merit but kissing the right backsides. Ireland is the ultimate bugger you mentality. It is a parody of the Red Flag anthem; 'The working class can kiss my ass; I've got the boss's job at last'.

Then again, who am I to offer such insight; a lowly little gurrier like me? A child who had to be abused daily, worked for profit; used as an industrial unit year after year and for what? Being involved in what was little more than a mischievous prank. This had set on its tragic course an over zealous police force, a cold-hearted sanctimonious judiciary, and a pack of wolves in Christian sheep's clothing.

Did this make Ireland a safer place; did it add anything at all to its standing and its reputation? No, only to the wealth of a tiny few whose shame stains the walls of their palatial homes. One day, unless they are already departed this earth their own Letterfrack's will open gates to welcome them into their next world.

My one overriding concern is that their callousness does not rot my soul as some of the potatoes I examine are putrefying. If that should happen then they would take the credit for spotting a bad one earlier.

This self-protective elite are manufacturers of bitterness and anti-social behavior; their mills turn out damaged goods. In that respect only the term industrial school has significance. Whatever anti-social attitudes may arise from the bitterness of our childhood experiences they must pale into insignificance when set against the crimes of their tormentors. Victor Hugo's *Les Miserable* was an account of tyrannical state abuse in France; it reared its ugliest of heads in Ireland too.

Chapter 9

Everyone has now returned to the industrial school from their summer holidays and all is quiet and subdued. The kids who had the good fortune to be able to go home had since been relieved of all the new clothes and shoes they had returned in. Policy was that you only wear Letterfrack school clothing. Parents had spent a great deal of money to proudly clothe their offspring that they might make the right impression upon their return to internment. These clothes were promptly destroyed; such Christian charity. The clothing could have been sent to good charities like St Vincent De Paul who would have made very good use of it but no, the clothing was used as rags for cleaning purposes throughout the school.

It being harvesting time there was the hay to be cut and we would file out to the fields. Instructed to stoop over so our hands and arms were outstretched towards the ground we formed up as a human hay bailer. We would then be stretched out in a single line stretching across the breadth of the field. Upon command we would all bend over and start collecting the hay by raking forward with our hands and creating a big wheel of hay that we pushed forward.

This work was unmerciful as you could spend up to four hours at a time bent over relentlessly moving forward whilst raking the hay. When we got sufficient amounts gathered some of us would be given pitchforks and we would then make the hay into haystacks. This was the one part I liked and always hoped I would be given the opportunity to build the hay stacks. We would spend all day in the fields and would feed on a lunch of bread and tea. I cannot recall ever being given water at any stage of the working day even though it could be very hot in the fields.

We would only be allowed about a half an hour to collect out bread and tea.

If you were not at the head of the queue then your break would be used up in the queue. The brothers were very strict on time keeping, especially Titch.

The hay stacks would grow on a daily basis until they began to take on the enormity of castles. Only then would the hay be collected before being stacked on a tractor and trailer to be taken to the silage pit. It was also stored in a big shed set aside for feeding the cattle over the winter months.

Some of us would be picked to go to the silage pit to trample the hay; I was always picked for this job. This was a big round crater about fifteen feet in diameter. The hay would be put in and molasses added by one of the brothers.

We kids would then trample around in circles as we stamped the mixture into the ground. The smell of the hay and molasses mixing was nauseating and it would be sticky under our feet.

We would walk in these treadmill-like circles for hours and days on end, trampling the hay until the pit got filled to near the top after which there would be more treading down to do; constantly stooping it was grueling and exhausting work. There was only half an hour set aside for a break each day. Far better a southern states plantation.

But at least the livestock would have good feeding from the results of our sweat shop labours. Likely they were thought more of than us kids for they had a bought and sold price; we never did and we were expendable. No wonder boys died there and buried in still secret locations. Certainly the cattle in the fields looked well cared for. They were certainly sufficiently well bred and husbanded for the purposes of breeding. Farmers from miles around would bring their cows to be serviced by our big strapping bulls; it was an awesome sight for a city kid to see.

Soon the days were becoming shorter in length as the late summer turned into autumn and leaves began to float to the ground; winter's warm coat for the tree roots. Dreading another winter in the fields I was trying to maybe get into a job in the tailors or carpenters shop but to no avail. There was no opportunity for applying for a particular posting; we all just got on with whatever we were instructed to get on with. So the fields and the farm and the bog too it was to be regardless of my feelings.

*   *   *

Each year one of the brothers would commission a play for Christmas and he would select a group of boys he thought were suitable for the required roles. This year I was picked to take the part of a Garda officer in the play; surprisingly I was over the moon at hearing this. I spent much time studying my part and other parts too and found this very fulfilling.

We would go to the hall in the afternoon to study and do the rehearsals. At least and for once we were treated as children and not slaves to the brothers' unique system of education. I really liked this acting thing and had done my best to learn every word and move; by this time I desperately wanted to be the best actor in the school; it would make me feel wanted and respected; twin joys never before experienced.

Coming up to the week before our big performance we were studying twice daily and this was followed by a dress rehearsal. One of the kids had been having some difficulty in remembering his lines and faltered a couple of times during the rehearsal. The brother in charge of the drama class, and who up to this part of the preparation had been open and helpful, went stark raving mad. He just lost it.

Dragging the then hysterical kid from the stage he took his leather out from under his tunic and started to belt shit of the youngster every which way he could.

Bang. Whip. Over the head, across his face and all over the child's body everywhere he could hit using all the force he could muster. When he was finished and breathing heavy from his belt-wielding exertions the poor kid looked like he had been in the ring with a heavyweight boxer for the full twelve rounds. He was bruised black and blue all over and weeping uncontrollably and pitifully.

Such an unexpected irrational outburst of madness frightened me and the other children to the core. It was made worse because we had looked upon this brother as a normal person trying to help the kids where he could. It was the sheer unexpectedness and uncontrolled madness with which he vented his fury at the youngster we found so disquieting. Alas, this brother was as mad and bad as was Chinney, Titch and the others. Each of them was branded with the same madness.

I still cannot understand why there was never an inspectorate; a solitary official appointed to ensure the wellbeing of the youngsters in the charge of the state. The Christian Brotherhood had literally been handed a license to act with the utmost licentiousness; to even murder at will. They took full advantage of their omnipotence

Needless to say the kid recovered somewhat but as certain the mental scars would remain for the rest of the mite's life. If it was consolation he was at least allowed to keep his part in the Christmas play. Suffer little children, come unto me indeed. We suffered and we came, and then we suffered again and again.

On the night of the opening the villagers respectfully and expectantly trooped in, taking up their seats on the right of the hall just as if it was a Saturday night picture show. It was apartheid at its best and most institutionalized.

Everything went well in the first half of the play and we had a break in which we were given lemonade and cakes that had been donated by the villagers. The second half went very well too and we received a standing ovation. The play ran to about an hour; when finished we were all so excited everything had gone so well on the night. I was hardly likely to be the one who wondered at what might have been the horrifying consequences had a major mistake been made by any of the kid cast. Would that brother have gone mad in front of the serried rows of villagers? I don't think so!

It was a great night and I couldn't wait until next year to play another part if I was privileged to be picked. I was cock o' the walk for weeks after the play. It seemed once again I had found a role in life worth dreaming for.

Chapter 10

As the year progressed and events surrounding Christmas and New Year became a distant memory nothing changed by way of routine. Up at the still dark wintry mornings; the hoar frost upon the trees; vapor rising from our nostrils as we wended our way to wherever we were destined. This began of course with the church service for nothing stood in the way of it. As Easter approached there were also the Stations of the Cross to attend.

Each night we would have the Rosary even if it was cut short but certainly a decade had to be chanted out loudly in reply to the brother leading the reading.

Religion was pumped into us at every opportunity; before and after meals, before bed and after awakening; in and after church at any chance that could be construed as a time of prayer. The prayers might well have been 'Dear God! Save the bog and all the fucking turf we can cut from it with the help of our slave kids.

Abuse by those in authority is often devious and imaginative; physical and mental; sexual and threatening. It is inflicted in many ways and pumping religion relentlessly into children, especially when they are lonely and vulnerable, is abuse of a different kind but abuse all the same. Theirs was a god who battened down on you; you never voluntarily offered supplication. I could never see how ramming religion down your throat without your approval could result in you embracing it and so the more I was subjected to religion the more I learned to hate it as a false god.

At Easter we never received any eggs of any kind; we ate religion and it ate us. We did get a long walk outside the school grounds on the Sunday. This was so refreshing and I always felt exhilarated after such walks. But this feeling of wellbeing was never to last long; the cold slap of reality hung menacingly over each day's routines.

It was so when on a bleak Monday soaked in mist and drizzle I found myself cutting the turf again, tossing the sods up the bank though if I had a weak throw it came bouncing back down on my head. This resulted in my once missing my step whereupon I slipped into the mire and was soaked through to my skin.

Brother Titch thought this great fun and was howling with laughter at the sight of me looking so pitiful. Dripping from head to toe with what looked like shite I was freezing and crying uncontrollably. A large sack appeared from somewhere and it was handed to me. Rubbing myself vigorously I was able to somewhat dry myself off but my clothes were still wet and my boots soaked; there wasn't of course any way by which they could be dried.

Titch for the rest of the day was in a great mood as a consequence of my discomfit. I refused to give in to his joy and continued work as best I could, feigning enthusiasm and bravado. Nothing would have pleased him more than to see me distraught and in obvious discomfit. Boy was I hurting inside and frozen to the marrow throughout the rest of the afternoon.

I presumed that after returning to the dorm, changing my soaking clothes and taking a shower for which I would receive a beating, I would feel and look better. It was a thought that heartened the ever optimistic me.

That evening my meal was wolfed down being far hungrier than normal. I could see some of the older boys looking at me in awe after hearing what had happened and how I had coped so stoically. This helped me to get over the episode and I was glad to be in such good health afterwards.

It also taught me that being heroic resulted in better results for oneself; something I would relate well to throughout my life. Whenever I was under pressure it was better to be brave rather than be an 'undecided' sort of person.

And so in life such things are learned without realising one is being taught lessons that help to make you a better or worse person in life. The mind takes experiences good and bad and after reasoning stores them until they are needed whether you like it or not.

The years I spent at Letterfrack Industrial School were to scar me for life; the constant uncertainties and the removal of the natural progression of decision making; a rite of passage for all youth passed me by under a welter of blows. As a result I was rarely able to hold a job or relationship down.

On the job part I was to end up self-employed and remained as such for the rest of my life. On the relationship part of life I was always looking over my shoulder for ghosts that might have never existed. They were however branded on my psyche to shape my character and personality. Not surprisingly I found it difficult if not impossible to place my trust in people and a deceit, no matter how small, was to open scars time after time.

This was something as a kid I found hard to comprehend; the meaning of trust or love. Each time I learned to respect and even like a Christian brother the weakness would be seen as a failing whereupon it was something to be taken advantage of. These two were learning experiences for each time I was betrayed my naivety was curbed and I learned to see them for the predators they were. So in life I would always try to put up a hard and strong front even if in my mind I was feeling weak and overwhelmed.

Things would have been so much better if Irish governments and the religious orders that held a malignant influence over them had done things differently. What an opportunity missed and to what advantage? Here was the golden opportunity to turn around the fortunes of the country's abandoned and desolate young people, to turn them into the greatest assets any country could wish for.

They had; the government and the religious orders, such wonderful opportunity to take these children; to then educate them to the highest standards. Instead they chose an ungodly course through which they squandered so many lives with their foul cruelties; their physical and sexual torture and unrelenting abuse. Paradise lost through predatory self-gratification.

Even though I lived through this appalling system in all its unvarnished wickedness to this day I still cannot understand why this was hidden under the cloak of convention. Why were they blind to the damage they were doing: Why couldn't one person see what was being inflicted upon thousands of vulnerable boys and girls over so many years that for them could be truly described as god-forsaken.

To the perverted and corrupt government and the religious orders, the so-called pillars of society, Ireland must have seemed heaven come early. Here was a pilgrim's end for the debauched and the shameless. Perhaps they were depraved enough to either resent the notion of an afterlife at which amends must be made; or they saw earth as a place to make one's own version of heaven. No doubt they are under the impression they would be given the all clear on their deathbed simply by confessing their sins. Why not? It is what they are taught and what they believe. Theirs will be a clean slate on entering the Kingdom of Heaven.

Given reflection it seems this is still the problem in our potentially great country. The haves and the have not's still live the life of the great divide that is hell-bound to continue in all its talent-sucking rapaciousness into whatever the future holds for it.

Can they see what is right under their noses or does the stink put them off? It is here in Ireland that our wonderful lyricists, our poets, dramatists and television agents need to focus; the home-grown whistleblowers.

They could so easily repair the damage and broken lives, restore Ireland's reputation. The ground has already been laid for them by Victorian philanthropists such as the founders of the Salvation Army, the National Society for the Protection of Children; scores of societies and foundations who then faced down that nation's abusers. Those here in Ireland who inherit their wisdom and sensitivities have the blueprint.

But back to Letterfrack Industrial School: Here we are again getting ready for summer holidays. It seems I might be allowed home as it has been some time since I did a runner. I haven't done one of those for quite some time and to the brothers I might appear to be a reformed character. I am hoping I can go to see my family for a couple of weeks. Their coming to see me is out of the question as my family doesn't have a car and public transport is non existent.

The only person who ever visited me was a former inmate. I recall his arrival in a red mini car which he parked outside the tailor's shop. We boys were all in awe of him; he was a big lad and dressed so well. We had only fleeting glances at him before the guards came to remove him from the school's grounds. It seemed the car had been stolen in Dublin; not good but equally ironic his reason for the visit. He was there to demand payment for sexual services rendered unto the brothers during his incarceration.

This focused our minds and there was much gossip between the boys as to who could drive a car and who could not. I was out of it: I was far too young to drive and in fact I had never given the matter a moment's thought. The rest of the kids fantasized that they were great drivers and were able to hot wire any car. Doing the rounds were many fantastic stories, no doubt dreamed up or exaggerated about lucky escapes, hair-raising chases; of how the Garda could never keep up with them.

There was a reason for their ineptness of course; the culshies were experienced only in driving tractors and horse driven carts.

Closer and closer the beckoning summer holidays. Having set my hopes on going home I reached the stage where I was presuming I would be allowed to. Had I learned it was to be otherwise I would have been totally gutted? Then, on the Saturday afternoon Friar Tuck assembled us in the yard where we were set in single rows. Having settled us he took out several sheets of paper from beneath his cassock. Holding them up and peering at the wording he began to call out names of boys, instructing those who heard their name being called to move to the front and form a single line.

This was the roll call of the boys who were to be allowed home for a holiday; the moment of truth. Confused and upset we had no idea if the names being called were those who were to be allowed home or were to stay. Such a cruelty was typical of the brothers; they never missed an opportunity to discomfit us. Why did they hate us so much? Was it a reflection of the hate they must have felt for themselves. Caught up in institutionalized horror were they victims too, like prison guards who become inured to suffering or see it as a perk of the job?

I heard my name ringing through the air and joined several others in the line. I was extremely apprehensive as from where I was I couldn't see a single orphan. They of course had no homes to go to so this could mean I was going home.

It took about an hour to call all the names and sort out the lines. It was then that Chinney came out of the door behind us and going to the front of the lines proceeded to announce those in the first two lines were going home to see their families.

We were each required to acknowledge we were being well looked after and were most gracious to the brothers for their care and support.

We would of course have said yes to anything at this stage: In reality we thought the life we lived there was normal and would see no reason in discussing our lives with others. Anyway, such was the constant humiliation that we were disinclined to discuss it with anyone; the shame being too great and God alone knows what the repercussions might be. We all know God can be deaf to the needs of children.

He leaves others to do that, and makes them accountable. I think that is how it works.

And so the Christian Brothers were safe; years of experience had taught them they were safe and anyway, who would ever place the word of a child higher than that of a Christian Brother?

I was exhilarated; it was three weeks to release and I could hardly sleep with excitement. Running constantly through my mind were the thoughts of what I would do when back in Dublin. I couldn't remember ever being so elated.

Those days and nights were interminably long. In the meantime there were trees to be dragged down and it was rumored that we were going to drain the large pond. It was more than a rumor for soon we were gathered on the bank of the mere near the doctor's house. It was about 9.30 in the morning; a glorious summer's day as I recall.

Two of the brothers emerged from the farm doorway; they were wearing their green thigh-high waders and soon joined our group. At the pond end was a sluice gate and they positioned themselves on either side of it. As they turned the ratcheted handle the pond waters began to escape to then rush down the hill in a torrent. It was an awesome spectacle and the stench was rancid.

It took several hours to drain and when it had done so the drained basin was filled with eels and fish flopping about in their distress. I had never before set eyes on eels that size; I think it was the first time I had seen an eel. One of the boys said: "They are conger eels. They can kill and eat you so keep well away from them."

Another said they were electric eels and the shock could easily kill you. My God, I was thinking to myself: Maybe they want us electrocuted and eaten to spare the expense of sending us on our holidays. Naturally I kept well clear of the creatures.

It was at this point that the two brothers waded in through the mud and silt and began to throw the fish and eels to the banks where they would end up in barrels put aside for the purpose; each of them having been filled with water. Our job then was to get into the drained pond and generally clean it of waste material; weeds, assorted junk and detritus. This was to take three days of back-breaking work; there was no opportunity to stand and stare as onlookers. Uppermost in my mind the passing of the days and with the passing of each I was increasingly excited at my imminent though temporary liberation.

After the pond had refilled, which took about four days, it was quickly re-stocked and it was a sheer joy to see the wildlife sporting about having been freed from their restrictive containers.

Their colors shimmered as they leaped and thrashed about in their natural environment. They seemed to be expressing a thanksgiving.

Other creatures were not as fortunate for some of the sheep were to be slaughtered. The farmer had explained to us how the best way to drift into slumber when sleep wouldn't come easily was to picture sheep; to imagine them leaping over fences and count them as they did so.

On this occasion he took one of them from its pen and quickly strapping its feet together placed it on its side.

Then, taking a large knife from his belt and holding the sheep's head up in one hand he slit the animal's throat from ear to ear. Then, kicking a bucket under the writhing beast he held it in such a way for the blood to drain into the bucket. Near satisfied that there wasn't much blood remaining he held the carcass up by its hind legs to allow the last strings of coagulating blood to ooze into the bucket.

Laying the dead sheep on its back and untying the foot strap he slit the belly open as had been done to the sow. Quickly placing his hands inside its still warm carcass he roughly jerked its entrails out to allow them to dry on the ground. The organs were separated and placed in another bucket. He then laid the sheep on its back and untying the rope that bound the feet he proceeded to slit the belly open. These he explained would end up as sausage skins. "Jesus," thought I: "These were going to be the skins of our fucking sausages?"

When the carcass had been thoroughly cleaned he then slit the skin at the top of the animal's feet and folding it over simply snapped each of the legs. Then, making his hand into a small fist he began to skin the unfortunate animal. Calling me over he showed me what to do and so I experienced the strangest of sensations as I felt my knuckles slowly slide down between the skin and the flesh.

When the skinning was completed the remains were placed on a wooden block and cleaved into portions. These were no doubt destined for the brother's kitchen where his daughters would be preparing the brothers' meals.

It was an amazing experience for a thirteen-year old child to see the workings of a farm and the slaughter of animals that you had hitherto seen only in picture books.

To discover that a sheep could be so easily skinned by hand was quite a revelation to say the least. So I took comfort from the fact that the learning experiences such as these would be assets in the future.

Other than that the school has caused me to regard authority as a threat, to never trust authority. From there on I would never trust or believe anything; at least view with cynicism and suspicion anything uttered by those who preach goodness and gods, or claim integrity. This is not an inherited wickedness or anything in my genes. I am sure a kindlier childhood environment would never have stained my thoughts or my soul.

When we leave the farm that day we went to the yard to wait for the call to supper. There I was pulled aside by brother Tea: "I want a word with you" he says.

I don't like the sound of this and I am very much on edge. My conduct has been exemplary; what could he possibly want with me? I am beginning to tremble when he smirks: "You are going home to your hovel for your holiday's boy. You just remember this. This is your home for some time yet so you be very, very careful with what you say. Things could get a lot worse for you."

"I know, brother, sir," I said quietly. "I am really happy here and I am looking forward to coming back."

"Good, that is what I wanted to hear from you. Now you run along for your supper is very nearly ready now."

At the time I didn't really pick up on the implied threat or even grasp the full meaning of his words. From a distance and given greater experience of life I realise its significance. It was their turn to be apprehensive as to what this little whistleblower might say when back in Dublin.

I have wondered since if there were stories about the industrial schools already seeping through the porous surfaces of society; if such stories were ever acted on. Back then I was interested only in my own survival.

It was July in 1965; a Saturday on which we were to leave came around quickly enough. Those of us lucky to be going home were up at the crack of dawn. We were each given a little bag with a change of clothing some shirts, underpants and socks to take home with us. We were excited knowing we had an early start as it was going to be a long journey.

The roadway at the top of the yard was filled with much hollering and good humored banter as the bus reversed into the driveway. Bawled into a line by Chinney we boarded the bus quietly for the brother was far from pleased at our obvious happiness. There wouldn't be much exuberance in the bus either as both Brother Chinney and Brother Titch was to accompany us all the way to Dublin.

Other kids went to other parts of the country; places like Limerick and Cork but most of the kids were from Dublin. Taking my seat at the rear of the bus I could hardly disguise my excitement. 'Here we go, here we go,' I was chanting quietly to myself as the bus's engine kicked into life and the driver put it in gear. The much looked forward moment had finally arrived as the bus heaved and jerked slowly towards the school gates, turned right and trundled along the main road. It was a long road of many tight bends but it was soon to pass Kylemore Abbey. The edifice looked almost Wagnerian in its solitude, sharply silhouetted and glistening against the lake and landscape.

I have since learned that it is a boarding school for better off girls and is run by a nun's order, but I don't think they would be abusing the little rich girls?.

I did wonder had they an inkling of what was going on just down the road from their impressive castle in its manicured grounds. Not that it mattered; they were quite innocently unaware of our plight and living conditions. Perhaps that is just as well: it is said that ignorance is bliss. I should imagine it is for knowing certainly wasn't.

The bus was fully occupied. The brothers having the front seats were smoking heavily whilst we sat in subdued silence. Things could still go wrong we supposed. Or, the apprehension had been replaced by another; the wonderment at what it might be like after such a long time to return to once familiar roads, locality and home. We had been told to keep our noise down; there was to be no fooling around so each of us sat quietly gazing out of the vehicle's windows. Each with our own thoughts as we watched the passing countryside. Perhaps we savored the welcome we were expecting?

As we entered Galway City we could clearly observe more people in one eyeful than we had seen during the previous year. They were strolling about in their short sleeved tops and the girls in short skirts. Some of the older boys were expressing themselves in colorful ways: "Oh boy; Look at that one," was commonly heard along with sharp intakes of breath and whistles from pursed lips. Isn't it grand to rejoin the real world? It is perhaps nature's balm that under the most trying circumstances we adapt to our new environment, even a threatening one, and forget the joys of freedom.

We arrived at Galway Station in good time as this left just half an hour before we would continue our journey home. Some boys dashed for the toilets, others among us waited patiently whilst taking everything in.

As we were all grouped together and in the care of the two bothers I suppose we were seen as an ordinary school outing party.

But to be sure the railway station's staff would know who we were; this much was obvious as the ticket master kept a very wary eye on our group. So he might for weren't we not convicted felons; criminals on leave?

Soon the steam engine pulling its string of carriages squeaked and hissed its way into the station and with a squealing of brakes jarred to a halt: "Take care you lot," we were told by one of the brothers: "There's a gap between the platform and the doors.

Like meek rabbits being herded from pen to pen we boys quietly climbed aboard. The rebelliousness I had felt when leaving the castle at the beginning of my sentence had long evaporated. That had since been beaten out of me. We were instructed to be on our best behavior. After all it wouldn't do for other passengers, the sanctimonious, to feel threatened by a little horseplay by youngsters.

No doubt they would be thinking quietly to themselves how outrageous it was that such lowlife being allowed out on holidays. The horsewhip would be far better for them and thus civilized order might be better maintained and the citizens might sleep more peacefully in their beds.

Clackety-clack, clackety-clack; the train picked up speed and the floor beneath our feet was beginning to sway as the miles to Dublin became fewer by the minute. Clackety-clack, clackety-clack as excitement built inside and many a bottom lip was chewed and a nose wiped on a sleeve.

At some point a few of the kids began to sing: "Were off to Dublin in the green, in the green, were off to Dublin in the green where the helmets glisten in the sun." This infuriated Chinney who bellowed: "Shut your mouths and keep the cackle down or you will be going back to where you have just come from."

Again quiet reflection resumed as the train rushed past clackety-clack, clackety-clack all manner of wonderful sights. There were trees in the fields and the man made rustic walls that reminded us of what was said to be now our real home at Letterfrack Industrial School. It made me wonder if we were passing similar 'schools'; a gulag chain of them?

As we passed we were startled by some of these strange looking buildings behind the stone walls. We couldn't help but wonder what lay beyond them; what remained hidden from passing society. How many had passed our own institution comfortable in the knowledge that it being in Ireland all was well with the world.

Occasionally we would hear the train's whistle wailing and as often the platform of a railway station would rush by. Some of us were playing cards; everyone was quiet and reflective; pondering the fickleness of fate perhaps. Knowing the natural high spirited nature of boys as a species I suppose we were oddly quiet to onlookers: That is if they noticed and could be dragged away from their own worlds. Of course other boyish groups would not be supervised by these two notorious brothers, and only we could know of the baseness that their notoriety was set upon.

The entire journey to Dublin took up nearly four hours of travelling time and passed off without incident. Neither I nor they would be able to think of the journey as long or short for to us it was timeless.

We were travelling forward but we were travelling back in time; between the mysteries of life with time being suspended during the train journey between Galway and Dublin. Ours was a vacuum, a nether world and a re-birth.

With much whistle blowing and the screech of tortured metal against metal the train entered and jerked to a halt as it hit the buffers at Kings Bridge Station. Instructed to stand we were addressed by Brother Chinney.

"You must be back here on Saturday week at half past eight in the morning sharp. You must be on your best behavior at all times. You are, remember, still under the control of the Irish state and must behave as such. This means no trouble of any sort under any circumstances. Do you all hear this?"

"Yes, brother!" we replied in unison.

"Off you go then and remember eight thirty on that morning, sharp." He bit the word 'sharp' off like he was snapping a bone in his teeth. Nothing changed his sour demeanor unless it was brightened by a child's discomfort. I had much to remember him by.

The train having finally coming to a stop I reached for the door handle. I had no idea what the welcome if any was going to be. Who will come to meet me; will it be my ma or my da? Will they be together or on their own?

Our file was separated from the rest of the alighting passengers and we walked up to the platform's exit from where even now I can see a group of people obviously awaiting arrivals. I think to myself that some of them look very much as parents look; impatiently and anxiously scanning the faces of the individuals, couples and groups of passengers now approaching them.

Then there are names being called out and much waving of hands in the air; it reminds me of the pictures you see of soldiers returning from wars. Fuck the brothers, I think as breathless I realise this is not a dream I have woken from; I am home in Dublin.

I am now running headlong down the platform towards the group of waiting people. The other boys are too and the parents are shouting and screaming, waving to them and encouraging them to come more quickly.

From the mixed unidentifiable mass of faces emerges that of my ma's. There she is, her face lit up by excitement and anticipation. I have no idea how I would have reacted to my father's presence.

"Ma, maaaaaaaaaaaaaa," I screamed with joy and like a silly Billy the tears started to gush uncontrollably. Although I am thirteen-years of age I am in a state of total self-destruction; losing control of myself as weeping with joy I fall into her arms and embraces. "Hush, hush, child," she murmurs. You're home now. Everything is alright."

I couldn't see her tears through my own, nor could I feel her sobs for I was sobbing too. Engulfed by extremes of emotions of joy I collapsed into her embraces. They were emotions of a kind I never ever want to experience again; not in this life or the next. There is only so much joy the human spirit can endure. I had reached my limits in my ma's welcome.

Chapter 11

It was one of those enchanting days when Dublin spreads out before your eyes; a beautiful city that embraces the River Liffey as it flows into the Irish Sea. Strolling along Victoria Quays, holding my mother's hand, was sheer bliss as we made our way home to North Great Georges Street situated to the north of the inner city. Our route would take us along the quays and over Capel Street Bridge into Capel Street. There throughout its length were dotted shops and cafes and a constant stream of passers-by.

I wondered if my face still looked tear-stained as I gripped my ma's hand even more tightly. Turning right into Jervis Street and then to Moore Street we passed through the stalls set out by the fruit and vegetable market traders; sidestepping people as we did so but hanging on to each other for dear life. Though it was now well into the afternoon they were still in full voice and again I heard the cries: "Bag of your best pinks here now, or fresh cabbage here. Just take a look at the shape and size of these bananas."

Perhaps the vendor herself believed the nutrient value of her goods would put all of life's ailments to rest. Ma stopped and bought some fruit before carrying on dipping in and out of the strollers, the gawpers and the buyers until we reached Parnell Street. From there it was only a few minutes walk past the Rotunda Hospital and Ambassador Cinema and then we approached the Town and Muck where all of my troubles had found their genesis.

By the time we crossed O'Connell Street, the scene of such savage conflict that would lead to liberation from occupation it might be wondered if for some at least it wasn't frying pan, fire. Is that what they meant when the officers commanding Britain's firing squads yell fire?

Finally we reached our tenement; the place I knew as home. Nothing had changed; not from what I could see. It was very much as I had left it and clearly the change was in me, and how profound that was.

"I have made you a coddle," my ma says gently as she sets about doing what mothers do second best; prepare food in the kitchen. A coddle is a Dublin stew. It is made by taking the household's biggest pot and into it goes the lot: potatoes, sausages, bacon slices, onions, white or brown soup mixes. It was a staple diet, especially for drunken husbands who returning from their revelry on a Saturday night found it easy to heat up and get down. The coddle is archetypically Dublin and of course the quest to get as bladdered through drink as was possible.

Pulling a rickety chair up to the small table my spoon was poised to mill the coddle. "Look," my ma says; "I have also got a batch loaf for you; it is straight from the bakery and still warm."

I think it was her heart's gift for she knew well how I loved the batch loaf; in particular what we called its heel, the end is normally cut thicker than were the inner slices.

Ma explains the kids are all playing outside and by now I have learned that my da is at work. He is back to being a coal delivery driver and ma tells me he wants a word or two with me.

"You know your older brother," she says; not so much a question as an affirmative. I do of course. "Well," she says: "He is no longer living here with us. There were a few difficulties with him. He has gone off to England. He has joined the British Army.

"Good," I piped up as ma placed the plate in front of me. I was starving and could have eaten a cow between two bread vans.

The news was exciting for me. Now he would be able to travel the world with the services, taking in all the sights and different cultures and lifestyles. It occurs to me that this might be a smart career move for me too. It certainly was food for thought as I wolfed down the food necessary for keeping body and soul together. Letterfrack at that moment seemed a long way away but not half as far away as it should have been. Here in the comfort and security of my own home its stark terrors were more clearly defined than ever before. Today it is as though I have woken from a bad dream for home is just as I remembered it and ma's cooking at its best.

"Yes, good for him says I between gulps before venturing outside to see what was going on if anything. I hadn't been sitting on the tenement steps for very long when a girl approaches: "Hi, what are you doing here?"

"Just dossing," Says I.

"Maybe you would like to go for a walk? Would you like to go for a walk? What is your name?"

I told her my name as I notice she is wearing a short skirt and cannot but help but look at her plump thighs and then her diddies. Her ample bosom seems to be trying to escape from her bodice-like top as taking my hand we set off to goodness knows where.

As we follow our feet my companion chatters non-stop about all kinds of shite that is going straight into one of my ears and out of the other without stopping. I will not be telling her I have come home from Letterfrack. Anticipating leading questions I have already hit on an idea: I will say I have been living near Cork with my uncle. In fact I did have an uncle who lived in Fermoy in the County of Cork so it was only half of a lie.

My new found friend thought I was delightful to which I could only ask myself if the girl was stark raving mad.

She hung on to me very much as my ma had done and I felt the stares of people as we passed by. By now I was feeling a little edgy and couldn't figure out why we were attracting so much attention. Nothing perturbed her as we completed our walk. I think she was a little put out when I disappeared indoors. She clearly liked my company although it was her who had done all the running; the walking and the talking.

The reason for the interest in me was revealed when full of curiosity about the attention I attracted I asked my ma. "Son," she says: "You have the most wonderful tan. You are so brown from the country sun; it is as though you have been on holiday. That is why they are looking at you.

My coloring was something I had never given a moment's thought to but after this explanation I took more notice of the complexions of others. It brought into sharp focus the white often grey pallor and beaten demeanor of my fellow Dubliners; the affects after decades following liberation from the occupier's yoke. Often silently these Dubliners shuffled about their business as they wandered from street to street; out of the grey; the grey being consumed by the grey; a people fog.

Da never came home before time was called at the public house he favored; later than that if he could get a 'lock in.' today, the day of the return of the Prodigal Son he was not to be moved one iota from his ritual. It was past midnight before I set eyes on him and in some ways was sorry I had. He was happy enough and his vocal chords were well oiled as making his way up the dark tenement stairway he sang his harmless ballads.

"How's my wayward little boy," he said as he peered at me. He was rocking slightly to and fro carefully picking his words as a man might warily find his way through a minefield. "Are the bastards treating you well, son?"

"Pausing for effect he went on: "Because if they are not I will be ringing their fucking necks so I will.

I will fucking kill them; all of them," he slurred as he slumped to the table's edge.

At that moment I knew that disagreeable that Letterfrack was this was not the alternative I needed. I couldn't exchange that for this. The memories came flooding back; the shared bedroom and the night pissing. Now I no longer wet the bed and can even get through the night without the need to piss in the piss bucket. How strange it is to share a bed I think to myself, aware of my brother's presence besides me as I drift off into a sleep.

Life goes on; I wake in the night to hear my father using the bucket. Pshhhhhhhhh and then, 'Fuck!' as he makes his way back and on his way to his bed flops in a chair. His bed is separated from mine only by a curtain room divider.

Early next morning I can hear me da washing in the sink. He clears his nose into the sink before getting dressed properly and heading off to work. I wonder how he would survive Letterfrack. My thoughts moderated with time. Granted he was always in work; always earning and reliable. If it meant he was equally reliable at drinking and getting drunk, and gambling too, then such was our herd instinct society there was little chance or encouragement to do otherwise. It was life; Dublin life.

The family were awake at this time and there are comforting sounds and odors drifting in from the kitchen. This morning the breakfast will be piping hot tea, batch bread and dripping. I love the dripping, especially when it is brown for I can then taste the juices of the meat that goes into the making of it.

My sisters and brother won't be going to school; it is their holidays too and they're quickly out of the house to do as other children do. Theirs is something of a different world for me; I have changed though like them I am still a child.

Perhaps it is because I have seen the raw sewage of humanity and it has colored different hues to theirs. I am still feeling a little strange being back home. I am also keeping a wary eye out for the girl I met yesterday; hoping that I don't bump into her.

When I do emerge from our tenement home my feet take me along Parnell Street and into Gardiner Street. There is a chance I will meet Redser there as maybe he is back home too. I do notice a lot of men grouped around street corners as I go on my way and wonder what that is all about. There is definitely an undercurrent. I can feel it and then I hear a word that is new to me: Scab!

I can see groups of men running towards two Lorries heading our way. The clusters of poorly dressed men, the lines of life drawn prematurely on their faces, are rushing madly towards them. They are calling out, 'Scab, Scab.' The

Lorries are being driven down Summer Hill towards Parnell Street and they are loaded with what appears to be bags of cement.

I watch startled and if anything mesmerized as in slow motion I see the lorries pull to a halt, their drivers' in fear of putting men beneath their wheels and them clambering over the bonnets and grasping at the vehicles' doors. All the time they are shouting; "Scabs," and "Northern Ireland bastards, robbing our fucking jobs."

The drivers are roughly hauled from their cabs, which is probably for the best as within moments both of the Lorries are torched and flaming furiously.

There isn't a Garda to be seen and not a sight of a fire engine either. I listen for the sounds of their imminent arrival but I hear nothing at all except for the rough voices. This is the tapestry of our times and our country. There is perpetual unrest, a simmering resentment at the misfortunes of life. Men born with aspiration find themselves seen as expendable. Such outbursts as these represent the fabric tearing at the edges. Their lives when born are celebrated yet they leave the earth unfulfilled.

I leave the mayhem behind me; I am motivated to go on my peaceful way by Brother Chinney's departing words about keeping out of trouble. My nose is clean so far. I want it to stay that way. The feeling of liberation as I walk where I want is a sensation I am still coming to terms with. Although I am aimless I am free. Perhaps one has to lose one's freedom to experience the intoxicating consciousness of freedom; just to cross the road and gaze into a shop window or to decide on a whim to take one road rather than another.

I didn't bump into any of my mates on that first day of liberation day but no matter; I was content enough to be home and to at least be patrolling their everyday environment. Those thoughts alone made me feel a part of real community again. I was no longer an outcast, an exile to be used and abused; my everything and all decided on by others who were more remote than would be foreign occupiers. If I felt alienated at Letterfrack and indeed some sections of the ruling class it could only be because our lives were being run by aliens.

The weather was kind. It was one of those balmy summer days when no matter how difficult one's life may be, no matter how dark the future, hope springs in the human breast. Dublin is the loveliest of cities. It is compact so you can walk from one end to another in no time at all and without feeling betrayed by tiredness. It didn't matter that I had little money. Where was the need? I could enjoy so much that money cannot buy?

You cannot go out and purchase the keys to your cell doors. You cannot lean across the counter and say, "A nice sunny day please," or tell the assistant you would like a portion of euphoria. These are beyond price; they are a gift denied to only those who either cannot see them or take them for granted. I saw and experienced them; not once did I take them for granted.

And so this day I follow my feet to Stephens Green, along Grafton Street and follow a route that takes in Dame Street, Halfpenny Bridge, which is called so as it was at one time a toll bridge that strands the river Liffey: I wonder how it got built its a lovely bridge done in iron and timber.

By the time my small feet have negotiated Jervis, Talbot and George's Street it is time for me to take my seat on the tenement steps; this time with a bottle of lemonade. Wasn't life grand indeed!

"Well, the fucking dead arose and appeared too many."

Surprised I turned on hearing the half familiar voice to find Redser standing there as bold and brassy as ever.

"Jaysus," I retorted: "You frightened the fucking life out of me. Just watching the world go by. How the fuck are you, you little shite?"

He told me he was fine and presumed right as he mentioned my being home from and on holiday. I told him I would be here for the next two weeks.

"Me too," he mutters darkly: "From Dangein. The fuckers only give us ten days though, but it is grand anyway. Are you doing anything later?"

I told him I had nothing planned as yet to which he replied that he had a little job in mind, if I was interested. 'Shite,' I am thinking; 'What kind of a little job?' I asked him what he had in mind.

"Well, we have the keys of an old boy's car and we're thinking of going up to Southside; smash a window and get our hands on some goodies. It is all the rage now. You just get close to a big fucking window, throw a brick through it and Bob's yer uncle, its called smash and grab."

"No I don't think so. Maybe me ma is going to take us to the Brue to play some games and hang out. She says it'll do me good to be seen with better people." No way I think to myself; no way am I going to get into this fucking mess again.

"Go and ask my bollix, you little shite then; and don't come calling to me when you need some friends." Says Redser.

With that parting shot he lit a fag and puffed smoke rings into the air defiantly. As he did so I turned on my heel and went up to our room. There, mother says she has the dinner just about ready. We are going to have eggs and spuds and then adds that she has saved some of the batch loaf especially as she knows I love dipping it into my egg. Music to my ears I think to myself.

After dinner ma did take us to the Brue. It is only a tenement but far better than ours and when one crosses the road to it one crosses a social dividing line. There she speaks to the manager about my attending during the evenings for a little while; he thinks it would be a good idea.

The Brue is a boys club run by yet another religious order of which there are many. The theory is that only street children leading disorganized lives get themselves into trouble. The devil is notorious for making work for idle hands.

They provide the club to get the kids off the streets and offer inducements like table tennis, rings, board games and card games to keep us amused. The rest of the boys are friendly towards me and there is a courtesy about them which is a little different from much of what I have had to get used to.

I settled in very nicely and was made to feel like one of them from the word go. I was quick to make friends and was asked if I wanted to be the fourth player in a game called don. It is something along the lines of bridge but this version is for the lowlife; the criminals and those on the edges of society.

One evening while awaiting my turn to play rings I overheard a group of about four older boys talking about some lady.

They were going on about her Mary being black and hairy and just like steel wool.

They caught me listening and one of them said "are you ok young one?"

"I was wondering what a Mary was". I replied

They all started to smile; have you never heard of a Mary before? No says I.

"Well it's a Mary McGee. And this one had a big black one with hair as thick as steel wool"." Oh says" I "but what is it"?" A Mary McGee is what girls have between their legs they all say in unison" and start laughing.

These events; the strolling and the club, provided me with the space I desperately needed following the misfortune. On the Saturday da told me he was taking me out to buy me some new clothes after which he would be taking us to the races.

Finding myself in Guiney's again I was quickly fitted out with some new trousers, shirts topped up by socks. Then, with the parcel tucked under my arm we set out by bus to Leopards Town and the races. Again it is the loveliest of days and everywhere there are crowds of nicely dressed people milling about. Up on their little wooden platforms the guys in their brown coats shouting out the odds; taking the bets, offering advice and taking the offered notes.

Me da joins the queue in front of one of these fellows and handing over some money takes tickets in return.

Then, making our way to the stands we find what is the best spot for watching the horses break free from the boxes. There in the stands there is no end of old ones dressed to the nines; all wearing their funny hats. It seems to me the older blokes don't look much better in their top hats and striped trousers but it sets them apart from those like me da; some wearing flat caps whilst others are bare-headed. To the blokes in the brown coats they are all the same as is the money that changes hands. In this respect there is no class distinction in money. It goes from the rich man's hand to the pauper's and back again; but the latter will normally have to count not only his change but make sure all his fingers are still there too.

"They're off!" I heard the piercing shout which lifted everyone up off their seats; the ones who were sitting that is. There's a stampede towards the front so everyone can get a better sight of the horses as they pick up speed and race neck and neck along the course route. I nearly went head over bollix in the rush forward but da held on to my arm tightly. Everyone is hollering and screaming their numbers, as if the horses could hear and take note of their wishes. Maybe their remarks were aimed at the riders: "Come on number whatever; you dopey ejit. Come on; get your whip out, you dosser!"

Soon the horses are hurtling along at breakneck speed and into the last furlong. At this point the crowd are in a frenzy of excitement. Even my da is screaming: "Get up there; get up there, you lazy fucking nag."

With the first three across the line there is a roar of disbelief. There is confusion as to how the closely run race ended. At the finishing post with hardly a nose between them there were three horses. The general clamor is dominated by the constant exclamations demanding who the fuck won.

"Quiet now," says the steward disapprovingly. "This has been a photo finish; just have a little patience if you will."

Everyone is edgy; stepping from one foot to the other, biting their bottom lips and clearly agitated. Then the near silence is broken by a roar. The outsider placed 16/1 has won the race.

"Jeysus be damned," I've got the fucking winner," says my da: "And I went and put the fucking bet on which way. But no worries, boyo; we are in the money."

There were a lot of sad faces in evidence and endless tickets ripped to shreds and thrown contemptuously to the muddy foot-marked grass. Dad on the other hand had a big self congratulatory smirk on his face as he queued for his winnings. There was no reason to wonder why he was so elated.

After alighting from the bus he was straight into the pub leaving me with the parcel under my arm and a ten bob note in my pocket.

"How did you get on?" asked ma when I entered the flat and placing a kettle on the hob took my parcel from me to examine its contents.

"I think he won," I told her, not quite sure what it had all been about but knowing da had left Leopards Town with more money than he had arrived with. "He's in Cusack's bar getting drunk I think."

"Oh well; easy come, easy go," she replied, probably thinking 'a fool and his money are soon parted' or words to that effect.

Immediately following dinner I went across to the Brue for a game of cards and after having my best night ever arranged to meet four of the others for a trip out to the Bray the following day. Later that night I, and the rest of the tenement, could hear the old feller making his faltering way slowly up the tenement steps.

He was singing his head off and on this occasion it was his favorite; the policeman's song. It was either that or a recital of 'The boy stood on the burning deck.' He had not the slightest concern for those who were disturbed by his drunken entry. Many of the neighbors were afraid of him and could be forgiven for thinking discretion being the better part of valor.

After a lot of failed attempts to remember the words or the order in which the song should be sung, the chorus being provided by my ma's nagging, he was finally edged towards the bed upon which he fell and was soon snoring loudly. He was the only one of the family who snored and so there would be precious little sleep for the rest of us; especially as the silence between snores was broken by his breaking wind.

Next morning I asked me da how he got on at the pub and if he had a great time. He told me he had but told me too; 'that fucker Lugs Brannigan was outside with the Black Maria and was going to rush the place if we wouldn't all piss off home as it was way past closing time and we were all still in there.'

Was this the right time to ask him for a loan? I was hoping he had forgotten the ten shillings he had given me the day earlier. "Da," I said: "I am off to Bray with some of the boys from the Brue. I need the train fare and some spending money."

"Wait and see, son," he says: "I'll just see if your ma has left any money in my trouser pockets. She's worse than a pickpocket when she gets busy."

"Here," he says as he hands me two half crowns. I have to admit that when he has some money he is free with it. This goes to the core of my ma's problems with him for he buys all and sundry drinks at the pub.

"Mind how you go with those Nancy boys," he says. "You keep your back to the walls; they're all tossers."

I told him they were fine and the only difference between us was that they spoke a little different. I hesitated to say they spoke better. That might in his eyes have marked me out to be a Nancy boy too. So it was that I went off in the direction of Westland Row where we were to board our train. The weather being so fine it was not surprisingly the train was full to standing room only as it rushed through the Irish countryside towards the little seaside town of Bray.

It is a favorite haunt for families who like to spend their free time gazing out at the sea or strolling the streets and waterfront.

For me and the others it will be the amusement arcades and I, because I still had the ten bob note and I am not short of spending money.

I am not a gambler as such but it is fun trying my luck on the slot machines; rising to challenges or testing my skill. The machines are usually cleverer than I am though.

It was while we were in one of the bigger centers that on a whim I decided to move my ten bob note from one pocket to the other. Unknown to me a girl was watching as I did so. After trying several games without any luck we stood idly around wondering what to do with ourselves for the rest of the day. The first I noticed her was when she approached; introduced herself with a 'hi' and asked me if I was new to the town.

She is a good looking girl with deep auburn hair reaching down in waves to her shoulders. She is wearing a pink top, a short white skirt and a pair of light white flat-healed shoes. 'Jesus,' I think to myself: 'Isn't she so beautiful. What Christmas tree did she fall off?' I was wondering what on earth she could want and was soon to find out.

"Where are you all going," she asks. We told her we were going up to the head for a stroll. That was the usual thing people did when on a day trip to Bray. Walk up to Bray Head.

"Can I come with you?"

We five boys looked at each other with raised eyebrows. Then, without hesitation other than our expressions we told her we would love to share her company. And so off we went with the girl tagging along besides us chatting away amicably. The questions between us flew as we learned a little about each other. She was older than any of us; at a guess nineteen or maybe twenty-years old and she has an inner city accent.

As we walk along side by side I can feel a warm glow from the closeness of her. On occasion she pulls a little ahead and I get the perfect view of her shapely long legs and her tight little bum swathed in the cotton fabric of her skirt. A sailor might have described it as two eggs in a sweat rag but for all of that a delight to the eye.

After a while we paused to give our legs a break and chose rocks to sit on; the grass being moist even in the fine weather. The girl sits a little in front but facing me. Her long legs seem to stretch out endlessly in front of her. I notice her diddies are not well developed but a nice handful I am thinking to myself.

We chatted together for a wile before setting off once more on our stroll. I couldn't believe my luck that such a beautiful girl was taking an interest in me. We hadn't gone far when she discreetly took my hand and stretching a little whispered in my ear: "Shall we pair off for a little?"

Again, I can't believe this is happening to me. I am under no illusions; I am not the best looking in the group and a couple of the others would I thought be more appealing to the girl. My only asset was my tan but that was about all.

I agreed of course and turning around to the lads I told them we were taking a break; we two would catch up with them a little later at the bottom.

There was the expected looks between themselves and a snigger or two but they were amused and no doubt wondering how I managed it. They wished us both a good walk.

I am on cloud nine as I stroll along with my little 'film star'. I am quite sure that other blokes with their girls must be turning and envying me. Inside my pocket there is a packet of fags and retrieving them I offer her one. I couldn't help but notice how long her slender fingers were as she thanked me and took one of the cigarettes. Her nails are painted a bright pink. I had never seen that color on nails before.

Happily puffing away it was at her suggestion that we made our way to a nice little cove we could see off to our left. It was a shaded area with ferns waving gently in the light summer's breeze. Here there was privacy from prying eyes and not once did it occur to me to question the happily unfolding events.

Lying closely together on the grass I was resting on my elbow and absorbing her beautiful contours whilst reflecting on how softly she spoke not to mention the magic of her eyes. She is breathing softly and I am getting what might be thought of as a mild orgasm just by being in her company. I have of course been close to girls before but never as beautiful and as affectionate as this one. I was experiencing sensations that were quite new to me and my heart was skipping a beat or two as we lay besides each other and talked. The sun was warm on my back and was dappling her face affectionately; just as I would like to do.

"Would you like to ride me?"

She came right to the point didn't she? Ride her? Jesus! How the fuck am I going to ride her in a place like this and right out of the blue like that. I had never heard the expression foreplay. What could I do? Dumbly I nodded and thought I would say yes and just go with the flow as you do.

They say it is as easy as riding a bike so I can ride a bike too; problem solved. With luck she won't realise I have never ridden a girl before.

"I would love to."

I couldn't help but wonder if she detected the near stammer in my voice as I wondered where the hell we go from this point. As I lay there bemused she repositioned herself slightly and edging her skirt upwards I could see her white knickers were clearly in view. Oh, there was no happier bunny than me but she has noticed I am uncertain and acting somewhat awkwardly.

"Have you done this before," she asks.

"Yes!"

"Spoofer! She laughs. Tell me what you do next then."

Fuck, I think to myself. What do you do next? She knew the right questions to ask didn't she; surely there were better ways to lose one's cherry than under these circumstances.

"I come over, you turn around and I stick my Mickey up the softest bit of you," I whispered to her.

"Up where," she asks suggestively and I can see the slight seductive controlled smile edging her lip. She examines my features with what I think is amused affection. Shite! Should I say, up your arse? Oh what do I do? Help!

"Well, maybe I have not done this before," I concede

Okay," she whispered alluringly. "I can teach you but the lesson in lovemaking will cost you."

"I am not sure what you mean; cost me?" At this stage my Mickey is brittle hard and throbbing; a state of near ecstasy she can't be unaware of.

"It will be ten bob and I will show you," she murmurs quietly, positioning herself as though it is already a done deal. "Come here," she says: "Give me your hand."

Taking it she guided it into the top of her knickers and I find a little slice of paradise as I fondle the clutch of pubic hairs and the moistness in between her thighs. By this stage she is having a good moan so has clearly discovered paradise too. But there was a price to be paid if the gates were to be entered. Taking my hand out of her knickers she told me it would be ten bob if I wanted it to go any further.

"I don't have ten bob."

"Yes you do," she replies: "It is in the right hand pocket of your trousers. I saw you put it in there when you were in the arcade."

Would you fucking well believe it? This isn't love at all. All she wants is the ten fucking bob in my pocket. It sure rained on my parade and I was so deflated that my Mickey became deflated just as quickly. By now she has seen the disappointment writ large on my face and is set on trying to save the situation from collapsing as quickly as my Mickey had. Moving over she kisses me gently on my lips. I am dumbfounded by the changing events but I do at least respond; it is the nicest of sensations as her lips gently brush my own. Is paradise beckoning again?

Tugging expertly at my trouser zip she reaches in and recovers my flaccid Mickey saying: "Oh, it is one of those is it?"

With that she began to rub some life into it with her right hand whilst with her left she produced from somewhere a paper tissue. Talk about coming prepared! Placing my hand back inside her knickers I do a little exploring and this time it is me that is doing the grunting and the moaning.

The pace quickened and oblivious to whatever else might be happening in Bray that day I responded to the occasion by urges that were well beyond my control.

Horrified, she is up on her feet and squealing that I have got my spunk all over her brand new skirt.

"You should have told me you were coming," she said, her voice was high with indignation.

How the fuck was I to know I was coming. I had never done this before. It was far more than my virginity that I lost that eventful day but perhaps it was another of life's lessons learned. Why should the ride be always so bumpy I thought?

Picture me; lying there abashed with my Mickey again flaccid, dripping the after cum as she swings her handbag, a blow that catches me on the side of my head before storming off up the hill. As she did so the rest of the world returned to sharp focus. What should have been a deathly silence was interrupted by an almighty roar; a cheer had erupted accompanied by much hand clapping. Looking upwards to the skyline over the small cliff's edging I could clearly make out the silhouettes of the boys from the Brue enthusiastically giving me a round of applause for my performance.

"We saw it all and heard it all," they are chortling: "Wait until we tell everyone back at the Brue."

I suppose it goes without saying that I dejectedly sat on my own during the long train journey home to Dublin and I never again set foot in the boys club.

But all in all I was not too put out by this episode I had learned a few things especially about the fairer sex. You need money for this sort of girl. For them it's all that they are about. I had also learned how to wank so not a bad investment in time and I had held on to my ten shilling note.

The rest of the week's holiday passed without any major upsets and Saturday came around all too quickly. The light at the end of the tunnel had been less bright with the passing of each day. On the day of departure I was up at 7am for we had to be at the train station an hour and a half later. Ma was to accompany me; this was in more ways than one the reverse of the walk we had taken two weeks earlier. My mood was not good.

The weather was fair and as we made our way along Moore Street the stall holders were all in high spirits. Their stalls were bending under the weight puff produce ready for the busiest day of the week. It was too early for customers; many would be still in their beds.

I was downhearted at leaving home again but knew there was no choice but to make the most of it. If I kept my head down I might well be home again for a week at Christmas.

As we drew nearer to the station we chanced upon others who were returning with us. Oddly enough they were all in the company of their mothers; there wasn't a father in sight. I suppose it must be concluded that it would be collaborating in betrayal; I can see that point of view. Otherwise their role in life was to work, if they had a job. For many their life purpose was to breed children, which is not the same as rearing them.

Brothers Chinney, Titch and Friar Tuck were on the station platform awaiting our arrival. There we were separated from our mothers. The younger ones were crying and I must confess I was wiping away the odd tear.

"Don't worry," son," ma said reassuringly. It is only time and even kings cannot stop time from passing." Her comment was wise and was to stay with me for the rest of my life. Such is the power of words spoken in thought and compassion. What neither of us knew was that it would be another long two years before we set eyes on each other again.

Chapter 12

We were placed into our usual lines and head counted and learned there were three kids missing. As we stepped aboard Brother Chinney went to the Garda on duty at the station. There he would report the names of the kids who had failed to turn up. The train was delayed by thirty-minutes to give them a chance but it eventually pulled out of the station without them. Those boys were never again seen in Letterfrack but word was that they had been caught and were sent to Dangein to see out their time.

The atmosphere on the train was somewhat subdued for the return journey. Anyone who had fags was in the train's lavatory with the windows open as they smoked their brains out. I had a twenty packed of Players and was definitely going to smoke everyone of them even if smoke was to come out of my ears.

Clackety-clack, clackety-clack the train sped on its way to Galway City flying past fields and low lying hill. In our carriage there was just the haze caused by cigarette smoke. Titch is furious at our relaxed attitudes but being on a crowded train there isn't a lot he can do about it.

On arriving in Dublin two weeks earlier we had been dressed to look typically like a group of school kids with our neat hair and clothes. On the return journey we are a motley crew of all types of dress and hair styles. There were crew cuts, shaven heads; boys wearing kaftans and hipsters. There were all the colors of the rainbow in the shirts now being worn. Ours was more like a group of youngsters going on a rave but that was before raves were invented back then.

Jerking along at its best speed our train was rocking from side to side and it wasn't long before I began to feel a bit unwell.

One of the kids gave me a pint of milk he had in his bag, courtesy of his ma. "Here," he said. "Take this. It will put a lining on your stomach; settle it."

I had never before suffered with travel sickness but then I had never travelled so far as this before; just the one earlier trip to Letterfrack. After drinking the milk I seemed a lot better so had another fag. Fuck, these things are rotten I thought to myself but it's the thing to do as it is supposed to make a man out of you. And so you keep on puffing like a little dragon?

Reaching Galway Station we all trooped off with dejected expressions. As we left the station and headed for the bus we could see a number of Americans standing about with their suitcases. It was obvious they were yanks as they looked so different in their manner, dress and posture.

One of the men turned to one of the women in their party: "Look Muriel. It's them scallywags we heard so much about. Thank God we're finished in Salthill. Could you imagine that lot in our hotel?"

"Kept awake all night no doubt," the lady replied sourly.

With that one of the older kids released a huge fart and ran towards the bus laughing manically. No doubt the yanks were impressed with his anus tricks. On the bus we were again head counted as it pulled away on the road that led to Letterfrack Industrial School. In the bog and so it was but we were from Dublin in the green.

Sitting at the rear of the bus I was still working my way through my fag packet and where I was sat there were steps leading down to a back door. After a while I began to feel sick again and this time I couldn't keep it down and spontaneously vomited all over the place. I was as sick as a dog and felt sure I was going to die. The dregs of my stomach were self evident and by now all down the steps and I could see the carrot's in it even though I had not eaten carrots recently.

Wiping my mouth on my sleeve I had to travel in the back of the bus with my mouth stinking and the smell around me making me dry retch. Those boys who had been sitting near me had wisely moved forward along the bus and I was made to feel like a leper for the rest of the journey.

On arriving at the school the instruction was to go and fetch a bucket with some cloths and to then clean the bus. That was followed by a good slapping. Welcome back to Letterfrack I thought to myself. At least having my own bed in some respects was better than sharing with my brother but I still had a feeling of emptiness; I missed the comfort of his body heat.

For some reason I couldn't fathom out the two weeks at home in Dublin had changed me. I now seemed to be a different person; I felt much stronger and was looking taller after my break; I had matured a little. Was it my chance meeting with the girl in Bray. Perhaps it takes very little time to turn a young boy into a young man. I was now more thoughtful. The brothers seemed to sense the change in me and never again did Chinney invite me into his room.

After the usual ritual of rising early for Sunday mass and all the religious palaver stuff that went with it things got back to normal.

When home on my holidays I never went to mass and when I got out of this place I would only do so at marriages or deaths; otherwise the church had lost this lamb by default.

Ordered back to the farm I was working hard each day and all seemed to be going fine as the summer drew to its end? By then the nights were drawing in and there was a distinct chill in the air and which penetrated the thin clothing we habitually wore.

We were back to hauling rocks from one muddy field to the next, stacking up the big rock piles before carrying them over to a field boundary and there making a wall.

Thankfully I was not required to use the sledgehammer as others were. Breaking the rocks up was the hardest work imaginable.

It was grueling and extremely cold work. Titch clearly took delight in our miseries and would run up and down the line as we carried the rocks. As he did so, like a Japanese slave-driver he would scream: "Come on, you lazy fucking bastards. Move yourselves won't you?" As he bawled he would whack our legs with his cane stick.

It wasn't long before the hatred for him began to fester and grow stronger in my mind. I yearned; I dreamed and I fantasized about wrenching the cane from his grasp and giving him a taste of his own medicine. The only thing that stopped me was the recollection of what had happened to a kid who had done just that. All I could do was grit my teeth and hope that he would miss me with his mad swipes.

We were back in the hall during the evenings and Brother Tea was still the one in charge of this particular duty. He continued to glower at me with an incomprehensible look of pure hatred just as he had that night I had kept winning my table tennis games.

"Come with me, you," he commanded as he pointed at me. It was obvious from his expression he was in a blistering mad mood.

Following him from the hall towards the main building I picked up a large rock and held it behind my back. There was an inward fury at the injustice I was facing and the dark thoughts coursing through my head were that I had had enough of you, you fucking head case.

He swept through to one of the school's classrooms with me following behind. There were by now beads of sweat on his brow and he was licking his lips, probably salivating as he gripped the leather tightly in his hands.

This was the strap that we all knew was laced with coins so as to cause further damage and hurt. Was it my attitude that infuriated him? Did he sense I was a better and a stronger person than he was and this was his way of showing who was boss?

"Unfasten your trousers and drop them and bend over that desk."

Producing the rock so he could now see it I replied: "You try this and I will split you open you fucking sick pervert."

No sooner were my defiant words uttered than he let out an almost girlish scream and brought the strap crashing down on my head. From there on he tirelessly belabored me; there wasn't a part of my body that didn't feel the agonizing bloodletting blows. As he struck at me wildly he was panting and constantly changing stance; making sure the slashes and blows would reach every part of my body.

"You will never ever answer me back or try the likes of this again," he screamed. His voice was getting hoarse with his exertions. Over and over again he brought the strap down or swung it across my head, my body and legs. By this time I thought he had lost all sense of sanity. The devil had taken over him and whatever the consequences, if any, he was now out to kill me. Holding me with one hand the blows rained down from the strap in the other. Afterwards I was surprised he hadn't continued to beat me until life left me that night. And for what; he was driven by a sadistic bloodlust that could only be assuaged on a helpless thirteen-year old boy.

Afterwards I was never brought to the doctor and spent over two weeks in bed recovering from the beating. This resulted in me nearly starving as I would only get food when one of the brothers remembered to bring a tray; this was not very often.

They wanted to keep me alive, just. To this day I don't know if it was deliberate or designed to make my misery and hurt worse.

Instead of this episode making me more fearful of the brothers it had the opposite effect. By now I had decided they would have to kill me before I would succumb to any more of this battering. When I was better and back at work I considered again it was the time to get out of here. I now feared for my life and I had a real fear that if I failed to escape I would never be leaving the bogs but would remain in them in an unmarked grave. The brothers, as was later shown, not above murder. I now knew the right direction to head in. I had memorized the route from the time we had gone to Dublin and back.

The first survival trick was to arrange a cache of sweets for sustenance on the road. I would buy these from the shop, bought with the money my ma sent to me. My plan was to take sufficient food and sweets with me on my next escape. By doing so I would be able to stay out of sight in the fields for as long as possible; to travel further before having to approach houses for food.

My escape was arranged for an afternoon during which I had been sent back to the dormitory; the pretext being stomach cramps; I had remembered the window above Chinney's door and decided to get into his room to rob whatever I could that might help me during my escape bid.

There was no one else sick and so I had the dormitory all to myself. I knew that all the brothers were out at work or busy elsewhere. Creeping silently along the corridors outside the brothers' rooms I paused occasionally to listen for the slightest sound. Satisfying myself that each of their rooms were empty I then lifted myself up to the ledge above Chinney's room door.

As expected it too was empty and so I climbed through the widow atop the door and dropped quietly into his room.

My heart was racing and the fear of being caught was so real for I knew they would kill me if they were to find me in one of their rooms. I sensed then but know now that there would have been the most casual of enquiries. It would be presumed I had successfully escaped and just disappeared somewhere into the glens and bogs. The region was too vast to be searched, the resources too few and the will non existent. I would not have been the first or the last child to meet such an end. Why not; we were society's rejects and had no value whatsoever. The bogs stretch out for mile after secluded mile. They make the perfect hiding place for the disposal of one's sins.

Quickly rummaging about in his drawers I found cartons of Sweet Afton cigarettes and took three packets. I haven't the slightest idea why I took just the three packets but it is what I did. I also took a box of matches and then climbed back through the window leaving everything just as I had found it.

Creeping back along the dormitory to my bed I hid the matches and fags under my mattress. I was just about ready to make my departure when I heard voices in the wash room: Shit, I thought; I better get into bed quickly. Quickly undressing I slid under the blankets and holding my breath listened carefully. I couldn't hear voices but what I could hear was this strange sound like cloth rubbing against cloth. Then I heard Brother Mutton Head from the kitchen say:

"Good, good! That was very good lad and you are in for a big roast dinner this weekend. Now just lick it all off and we can get back to the kitchen."

Shite thought I; he's got some kid out there and they're doing something they shouldn't be doing. Putting my head under the covers I was hoping that if he looked into the dorm he would not see me in the bed.

After a while all was silent again and creeping silently out to the washroom I found it all clear; there wasn't a soul to be seen or heard. I could hear all the lads coming back from the fields and knew I couldn't take off now; I would not be able to get far at this time of day and would soon be caught.

Making my way silently back to my bed I decided to bluff it out if I was questioned about any missing fags. As luck would have it, and I needed some of that, Chinney didn't seem to realise there were packets missing. The next morning I feigned sickness again.

Leaving it until I knew everyone had gone to their work I slipped from my bed and putting on as many clothes as I could I slip out of the dormitory and down the stairs. Fuck! What was that? I could hear noise coming from the bottom of the stairs. Holding my breath I stopped before peeping around the banister. Peering down I could see Brother Friar Tuck standing in the main doorway. He was smoking a cigarette; his other hand was behind his back.

It was clear that this escape route was out of the question. His presence meant I either had to remain where I was and wait for him to move or cut through the other dormitory. I was not familiar with the other hall and wasn't sure I could get out through its far end. I thought it better to wait to see if the brother would move,

As soon as he finished his cigarette he tossed the butt out ahead of him and turning brusquely went back into the tuck shop. Here was my opportunity. Silently descending the flight of stairs and along the corridor I went quietly past the doctor's surgery and into the cloakroom. There I retrieved the food parcel I had stashed there.

This left the yard to be crossed and the only way to do that was to stuff everything up my jumper and walk casually across the yard as if it were perfectly natural that I should be there.

My route would take me across the yard and past the hall; to its far end and then I needed to take a left along the lane. At that point I would clamber over a roadside wall and into the obscurity of the field. My plan was to stay as close to the main road as possible. By this strategy I wouldn't get stuck in any bogs or lakes and so would make better time.

I could also listen out for cars coming along the road and be able to use the walls as cover. This time I was determined to get away; I was under no illusions as to the severity, even life-threatening beatings I could expect if I was to be caught on this second occasion. I was unlikely to forget the beatings and other punishments I had been on the receiving end of last time I had gone on the run.

I made it safe and unseen to the field from where I would start my solitary journey. Putting my best foot forward and squaring my chin determinedly I set out walking due east. After about half an hour's walking I heard the sound of a car in the distance. Ducking down behind the wall I waited for it to pass. Holding my breath I could hear its approach and then, after it had passed the spot where I was hiding, the sound of its engine being absorbed by distance. I was hoping I would be able to give myself five or even six hours head start before the brothers realised I had again gone on the run. This would mean I would be so far away they would be confused as to the direction I would have gone in or the distance covered. I was hoping I would be a very small needle in a very big haystack. My plan was to reach Galway, board a train and from there go to Dublin by hiding in the train's lavatory.

Rewarding myself with a cigarette I took deep drags but paced myself: I had no intention of making myself unwell. I hadn't had a cigarette for some time. It tasted good and I felt much better for it. Shortly after resuming walking I met what might easily be my nemesis. I was confronted by a biggish lake.

As it stretched under the road and which for a little way became a causeway I had to get my choice right. Walking around the lake would add considerably to the time I was taking but the distance gained between me and Letterfrack would be not that much greater for the hour or so it would take to get round it. Worse, it would make me a highly visible fugitive as much of its banks were in the open and clearly visible from the road.

I had little choice but to climb over the wall and sprint as fast as my legs would carry me until I reached the lake's far side. If a vehicle was to approach during my headlong flight it was the end of another bid for freedom. I would be seen and even if it was not a threatening situation the car would be sure to stop and question me; a small boy out in the wild country roads as darkness is beginning to descend. I presumed that in such a rural location everyone would know everyone anyway.

Off I went like the clappers of hell; head down; my legs going like pistons with my heart pounding and my lungs sucking in air. The wind was ringing in my ears as I reached the far side of the water's edge. I had just shinned over the stone wall when I heard a car's approach. Crouching down out of sight behind the wall I was holding my breath so I could better read the sound of the car's progress. Wonderful; like the earlier vehicle it drove on past, laboring a little as it approached the gently incline. From where I found myself I could see a small house, perhaps a smallholding off to my right. If anyone was looking out of the window or working in the front I would be clearly in view. I decided to take a chance; cross the road and make my way along the far side of that wall. It would shield me from the house.

With a run at the wall I again shinned over it but my plans were dashed when on reaching the far side of the road realised my route was blocked by a mass of overgrowth and wild shrubbery.

I had little choice but to quickly retrace my steps, use the wall as a camouflaged backdrop and just take my chances. At a half run whilst keeping my head down I covered some distance but as far as my feet would carry me the house remained in view. If I was close enough to see it then they were close enough to see me. It seemed an eternity before its outline was lost in the distance behind me.

Only then did I feel safer but I was in desperate need of a rest and a cigarette. By this time my thoughts were all over the place. Maybe I hadn't put enough thought into this. Uppermost in my mind was the reasoning that I simply could not afford to be caught and returned. I was sure that death perhaps; certainly serious injury would be my lot if those brothers could get their hands and their boots on me. I had no choice but to put as much distance as possible between me and them.

Pacing myself I continued on my way by following the line of the roadside wall which to me seemed a far better idea than trying to go across country. The only potential danger was my coming across a cottage or farm; they are naturally close to the country roads and this road was unlikely to be an exception. There seemed to be many lakes scattered along the road's route, which wasn't helping matters at all.

Darkness fell quickly and from every direction I could hear the sounds of nocturnal creatures. The brothers would by now be aware that I had disappeared and I could well imagine the hue and cry. They would already be getting excited at the thought of the punishment they would inflict on me upon my return. But, I was not going to be returned. They would be disappointed.

Some of the noises were to me quite strange and caused my hair stand on end. There was many a cold shiver that ran down my spine; many a heart-stopping moment as the night closed in.

Taking the philosophical view I comforted myself with the thought that they were more likely to be afraid of me, and what I couldn't see wouldn't hurt me. I was determined not to stop but to carry on through the night. Distance covered was more important than was rest. I knew the greater the distance the more difficult it was for their net to work.

It was very late into the night when I stumbled across a large farm. The dogs were barking before I could see the buildings but I decided to keep going. I was pinning my hopes on the farmer thinking it was only a wild animal causing them to kick up such a fuss. In truth I must have resembled a wild animal. Had he let them loose I would have shit my trousers because I am terrified of large dogs. I kept going until the sound of the barking faded into the distance behind me. Eventually I came across a little copse that looked safe and decided it was time to taker a breather and have a smoke. With a little bit of luck I would sleep for a little while.

As I lay there on my back, pulling the occasional draw from my cigarette, I could see the sky's dark bowl above my head. The stars were shining and twinkling so brightly and a sense of euphoric tranquility washed over me. Feeling drowsy I thought not to fight it and soon fell into an oblivion in which there was no fear; I was a not a fugitive in fear of his life and there were no brothers. Most of all, there were no brothers.

I have no idea what time it was when I woke with a start. Where am I was my first thought; where the fuck am I? Was this a dream, a nightmare? I was so cold I was shaking uncontrollably and I am as wet through with the dew I might easily have been thought to have fallen in a river. As I see the sun rising I have the sense to know that if I get to my feet and start briskly walking the passage of time will dry my clothes out. Lighting a fag I head to where I hope is due east.

Doubts were beginning to set in. Had I blundered? I am soaked through and my clothes are like rags; how on earth will I make myself presentable to board the train at Galway Station? Regardless and determined I set off at a jog. Before long wisps of steam were rising from me, which makes me chuckle. Now I am the steam-kid and I might become the cowboy I wanted to be. In my imagination I am Gene Autry, the cowboy screen legend and I am sure going to make it to that town yonder.

On I jog through the fields and for as far as the eye can see it is open land. My idea to travel overland keeping to the road without actually using it seems to be working. It wasn't long before my clothes were beginning to dry and time to take another breather and treat myself to a few sweets. The gobstoppers were keeping my mouth moist but were doing little to tone down my hunger. I also need something to drink and keeping an eye out for a stream it isn't long before in this boggy terrain I come across a clear running one.

Dropping to my knees I lap up the water as a dog does for this is no time for convention. Having satisfied my thirst I set off again. The hours passed and it was late afternoon when I chanced upon a large building I thought might be a church. I carried on past it; I had no desire to throw my need for charity on religious people; they would be as sure to hand me over to the brothers as would the Garda themselves although with comforting platitudes no doubt; strangely absent when the strap was torturing a child's flesh.

Although I am aware of a lot of cars using the road I am not too much bothered by them. It is over twenty-four hours since I made my escape and I must have covered a great distance. I was in no doubt as to the state the brothers might be in; children are usually captured and returned within a few hours.

By the time nightfall comes I am exhausted and my pockets empty of sweets. I hack on regardless. The more country miles I can put between me and Letterfrack the greater the chances of escape. The ground beneath my feet is getting harder and the boggier ground is behind me in the distance; could the reason be that I am getting closer to Galway City I am thinking to myself. The thought spurs me on.

I am jogging along in the darkness when I ran straight into the barbed wire fence and tumbled over and further into the entanglement. The pain was piercingly sharp and came from multiple places; the barbs had ripped my clothing and had torn my skin; the small wounds that were bleeding. I was badly winded too, as much by the unexpectedness of it. I can feel the blood seeping through my jumper and putting my hands down my legs I can feel the blood there also.

Clambering to my feet I haven't the faintest idea what to do: In my juvenile mind there is a real possibility of my bleeding to death out there in the wilderness. Was the brothers' job to be done for them by this misfortune? Had I only seen the fence in time? Trying to stem the blood by licking and drying my hands was clearly not going to work. I needed to find a stream and clean myself up properly. From here on there would be no more running in the darkness for me. The prudent way was to travel more carefully; accidents like that only slowed progress up anyway.

I had never known such hunger and the need for food is now giving me cramps; I am nauseous with need and sucking on the last of a couple of sweets I discovered in an inner pocket. The priority now was to look for a safe place where I might catch some sleep. Within half an hour I came across a small stone bridge crossing the main road. Ducking under it I realised it made the ideal shelter; I had tonight a roof of sorts over my head. This is where I was going to spend my night, curled up in a little ball. Perhaps the cover would keep me free of the dew.

Sleep wouldn't come easily. I was sore from the torn skin and it seems to be a lot colder than it was during the previous night. Looking back I realise this was on account of my extreme hungriness and exhaustion. I am trying to keep my mind from wandering as my thoughts are driving me nuts.

Might I die out here; will someone one day come across my body or skeleton in a little hollow and wonder who I am and what I am doing there? What if a wild dog comes along and finds me here? The night before I was tired but tonight I am completely drained. The night before I was exhilarated from the adventure but this evening I was lonely and becoming very frightened. I think I must have sensed circumstances were beginning to dictate the outcome.

I must have drifted into sleep because I was awaked by the sound of a tractor or a truck crossing the bridge just feet over my head. A few small pieces of earth dislodged by its passage showered down on me. Waiting for the sound to disappear I then crept out of my shelter. I was bursting for a piss and with my back to the road I take my Mickey out; the relief as the stream flowed endlessly. The sun is coming up; I can feel its warmth and best of all my clothes are dry. A lesson learned; don't sleep out in the open.

The hunger in me seems to have eased and hoping it doesn't return I once again set my feet in what I hope is the direction of Galway. It was later in the morning that I came to my first village and this presented problems. How do I get round or through it without drawing attention to myself? I was crouching behind a wall figuring out my next move when I heard someone shouting: "Hey, boy!"

Shite, I am thinking. I have been spotted.

The caller can only mean me and with that three rozzers came hurtling towards me, their long black gabardine coats flapping like batwings as they closed the distance between us. The look like the avengers of death.

"Hey, boy. Don't move. Stay right where you are."

Fuck this I think to myself. I didn't get this far to be caught and off I went as fast as my legs would carry me. I hadn't got very far, maybe a hundred yards during which I could hear their closing in on me. The grunting and panting was just over my shoulder when I was thrown to the ground as a result of the police officer's rugby tackle. Exhausted and winded I was no match for the burly policeman whose weight and strength pinned me to the ground whilst the other two closed in. As they pulled me to my feet the one who had rugby tackled me dusted his tunic off.

"Are you okay, lad?"

"I am fine, you big cunt."

The response from his open hand sent me once again crashing to the ground. I am dead now I am thinking to myself as I am roughly dragged to my feet and more or less dragged to the roadside. Clearly in view is the police car all liveried up with Garda on its sides. They must have seen me from the road. Well I am well and truly fucked up now because there is no way I am going to escape the clutches of these three fuckers. They are talking about me as if I'm not there.

"Little bollix! Did you see the state of him trying to make a run for it? He looks like a little knacker."

"He probably is one. We'll have to get him back to Letterfrack now."

"How old are you, son?"

"Thirteen; it will be my birthday soon."

"Well we just spoiled it," he said with a low laugh. The inside of the police car stinks with the overpowering smell of wet gabardine and heavy police uniforms and farts.

"So you are thirteen years old and planning on walking across Ireland? I like confidence even when it is misplaced." The other policemen snorted their approval at their colleagues' wit.

"He covered some distance; maybe twenty miles or more. I don't remember any others making it this far." The other one muttered that he had no recollection of a kid getting so far either.

"I wouldn't want to be in his shoes when he gets back," grinned the driver. "They will give him a good tanning for sure."

I am just sitting there, almost hidden between the two Garda while I am listening to this drivel. As the car sweeps up the road past the abbey I know it won't be long now before I am in for the beating of my life, literally. As the police car turned into the graveled driveway of the school it followed the lane passing the hall and pulled to a stop outside the tailoring shop. I am thinking to myself; these rozzers have been here to this exact spot before.

Brothers Chinney and Tea are waiting expectantly on our arrival. It was as though they were expecting us although I hadn't heard anything being said on the car's radio. It crossed my mind that there might be some way of divine thought crossing the miles; something that was yet beyond my understanding.

Jerking the car door's handle the door flew open and Chinney reaching in grabbed me by the scruff of my neck.

As he pulled me out he hurled me to the ground. He did so with such violence I thought my back must be broken.

As he did so the policemen climbed back in their car and without a backward glance spun the car around, sped down the driveway and turning through the gates disappeared from view. Their duty done, Chinney's was just beginning.

Before their car was out of sight Chinney had become demented and with his swinging boots was kicking out at me. I was rolling about the driveway trying to avoid his boots hitting me. Curling into a ball I was covering my head and my face as the soles and tips of his boots thudded into me.

"You bastard; you fucking little bastard," he is screaming as seemingly he is trying to hit me with every limb he has. "You are done for now. After all we have done for you this is how you show your fucking gratitude, you little bastard. All that and all you can do is turn around and run away again. Well I am telling you, this is the last time because I am going to break your fucking legs; see how far you can run then, you little bastard!"

At some stage Friar Tuck came running over: "That's enough now; that is quite enough."

Taking me by my hand he leads me across the yard towards the cloakroom. There he takes a towel and wetting it under the tap he begins to wipe away the blood and the tears from my face. "It's okay, lad," he says. "We'll soon get you fixed up, now hush your sobbing; hush, hush."

The brother then takes me to the showers where I strip off and step into the shower, while he goes off to get towels and some clean clothes for me. I am shivering with fear and pain; I am totally drained. I felt near to death. After that I am put to bed and he suggests I get to sleep and we will see how you are tomorrow.

I dropped off immediately and awoke the next morning to Brother Chinney's hand clapping.

When I rose from my bed everyone is staring at me in awe but nobody is saying anything. It was an uncomfortable feeling. I felt like some kind of freak. I just carried on as normal. Getting washed and dressed I can see my face is very badly bruised and there are big lumps on my head. There are bare patches where clumps of hair have been wrenched from my head. I imagine this happened during the frenzied attack by Chinney on me when I was brought back.

As normally I went for breakfast with all the other lads and I can feel everyone is talking about me in whispers and there's many a furtive glance in my direction. After the breakfast is wolfed down we go to the yard. I am standing at the door leading to the yard wondering if I have to run around the yard when Brother Chinney comes out behind me.

"Now, my lad," he says; "Run! Every time you come into the yard you run. You run as if your life depended on it because it does. Do you know what I mean? You life depends on you running. Do you hear me, boy? Do you hear me, you little shite?"

So off I go again, ever the lonely runner but I don't care as my freedom is not your world; it is the freedom in my head and in my imagination. They all saw me running around the yard. If I seemed to do so enthusiastically it was because inside my head I was running as fast and as far away from this dreadful place as I could. I was no longer with them. I was tearing across the fields and bogs reaching out for Galway City and my home city. I am constantly in a far away place in the back of my mind my dreams are mine and mine alone they cannot take them away from me.

I never ran in the school's yard. I ran for me and I ran for freedom; the freedom of the hillsides, the road and avenues of home.

I was never taken to the doctor to be seen for my injuries; nature and time was to be my only healer. So as on the earlier occasion, every time I entered the yard I have to run. This will go on again for months but for reasons I cannot fathom the first beating was not as expected followed up by others.

This happy state of affairs was not to last. There came the morning when I was called out of the classroom by Brother Chinney. Again there was no reason for me to be picked on. I had kept my head down and dutifully done everything that was required of me. There didn't need to be a reason for a beating; they were carried out randomly, on a whim or with some forethought: Clearly the brothers relished the occasions.

I was then taken over to the hall by the brother and made to drop my pants and bend over. Methodically he began to beat me across my bare buttocks with his leather. Holding my breath I prayed I would be able to withstand the ordeal without sobbing or crying out in pain. I bit my bottom lip and squeezed my knuckles together. Each stinging strike was like red hot metal tearing into my flesh. I was sure I could beat the bastard and imagined us as being in a fight; his intention to make me scream, my intention to not do so.

The strokes must have been tiring his arm as he swung the leather over his shoulder as to cause the maximum hurt. I could hear him panting and swearing under his breath as he belabored me. After a while the pain was so excruciating animal like whimpers turned into screams as I begged for forgiveness; screaming for my ma and begging his forgiveness. I was pleading, sobbing my heart out, and crying for him to stop. I couldn't take any more.

When he finally did stop all I could do was lie on my side and scream my pain and my cries echoed through the hall. As I did so he just stood with a sly smirk on his face, obviously excited by the effect his beating had on me.

"You be prepared to receive this type of punishment anytime I feel like giving it to you. You little bastard! I will stop your running you will run no more do you hear me" He screamed.

Yes. Yes brother. Oh God the pain was unbearable! Yes brother Sir I hear you, I will never run again. Please brother. Please brother!

After that beating it took me three days before I could walk let alone run. When in the hall I had to face the wall at all times. I was not allowed to mingle with the other boys; or to play table tennis or any other game.

I am running around the yard one day when Brother Chinney calls me over and telling me I need a change of trousers he beckons me to follow him.

Taking me to the clothes room he gives me a pair of pants that look like gophers; they are wide at the top and taper into drain pipes at the bottom. I seem to recall a bigger lad coming back from his holidays with them; part of a suit that had been hand made for him, they are grey in color with stripes running trough them.

When I pulled them on I looked like a circus clown for they were swimming on me. But this is what Chinney wished me to wear and wear them I must. Whatever it took he was determined to break my spirit and so I did whatever was demanded of me as I had come to fear being beaten. There was no respite in my sleep either for my dreams was of being beaten, or of my running; always running.

I wore those pants for about a month until Brother Friar Tuck was in charge of the yard and one day he called me over. "Who gave you them pants to wear?" he asked as his eyes challenged my own.

I told him. Shaking his head he told me to go to the tailors and to tell them I needed to have a proper fitting pair of pants. This I did and felt so relieved that all the laughing and sniping from the other lads would from there on cease. It was one thing to be forced to run around the yard but to do so looking like a clown was just too humiliating.

My happiness was not long lived as the very next day Brother Chinney was on duty and it didn't take him long to spot my change of trousers. "Come here, you," he yelled. "Where did you get the trousers from?"

I told him that one of the brothers had told me to get them from the tailor's shop to which he replied that I had better go back to the shop and exchange them for the ones I had taken to them. On arriving there the brother in charge said they had since been cut into cleaning rags.

I told Brother Chinney what the brother in the shop had said and the words were barely out of my mouth when his boot swung up and the toecap of it plunged unexpectedly into my stomach. I fell to the ground reeling and holding myself in the most terrifying pain. I had no idea anything could have hurt so much. I was sick, retching, throwing up and gasping for air. I was so badly hurt I thought I was about to die. As he grinned at what he had done I was contorted in agony, rolling around the ground clutching myself and being sick. It was like I was drowning; the sensations were beyond all my previous experiences; I was drowning in pain.

"Get up. Get up you little bastard," Chinney screamed at me: "Get up and get fucking running."

I couldn't get up. I was vomiting and in the most terrible pain. He went hysterical; screaming and swearing that I should do what I was told. Other than gasp gulps of air and hold myself I was helpless; I couldn't even stand let alone walk or run.

With a look of utter contempt he turned on his heel and left me writhing in my misery.

I have very little idea of how long it was before I could finally stagger to my feet and for what remained of the day I could only limp around the yard holding my guts. All the time I was praying he wouldn't return and make me run. I couldn't take any running and nor could I take another beating.

That night I found it so difficult to get to sleep as every time I tried to drop off I felt like I was not going to wake up; I still had this sensation of drowning. The days were just running into one endless time capsule as I tramped around the yard. The feelings of desperation and loneliness were getting so bad I no longer knew how to handle it. I felt I might be losing my mind.

How long more was I going to have to run? When would they think I had been punished enough? When would this stop? Would it ever? I know running away was not allowed but what was to be done? Was there no one to stop and figure why we ran? Did I have to stay and be abused on a daily basis; is it not built into the human psyche to escape and to run when it was a matter of survival? I had no idea but I do know that my life was being changed beyond all repairs in this hell hole.

I was not invited to take part in the Christmas play that year. I was to attend it facing the wall in the hall; my running was to be extended well into February. This was the longest period of punishment running in the school's history so I was led to believe. I was been called 'The Runner' by the other kids.

I overheard some of them saying to a new kid one day "see yer man over there he's the runner the lunatic runner"

If the Brothers thought this would deter me from running away again they were wrong.

I was forever looking for opportunity and as soon as it presented itself I would be away again, haring across the countryside to nowhere in the full knowledge that escape was impossible but attempting to was not

Being beating regularly didn't seem to work; not in my case. It only made me more determined to be rebellious and as often as I had a chance I would do wrong if I could. Each time I did it was payback time for the system I was enduring.

When the running finally ceased I again kept myself to myself. I didn't feel close to any of the other kids. All I wanted to do was do my time on my own. Feeling that being a loner was better than being caught up in the problems of others my decision to be an outsider was to help me get through this very troubled period in my life.

Chapter 13

Digging up the turf again this year was horrendous and there were cuts, scrapes and bruises all over my body. The slightly less arduous job of actually cutting the turf was denied to me as it was thought it might give me opportunity for fleeing again.

It was no problem for me; I just gritted my teeth and got on with it. The clock was always ticking away in my mind that the day would inevitability arrive when they could hold me no longer unless they buried me in the bog as they probably had others.

The work on the farm was hard; it was cold and wet work, which the body never really adapted to. As a consequence my heart still goes out to children whose situation requires them to work in similar cold and wet environments.

Later I was put back on the early morning milking duties. This work means more or less around the clock animal husbanding. The cattle needed to be brought in from the fields and then the need to milk them dry. Then there were the buildings, not just the cowsheds to be cleaned. By the time you had done all this it was afternoon and the process had to be repeated. There wasn't a break as such. Between morning and afternoon milking we would be given other chores to keep us occupied. The farmer's view was that time wasted was time lost. It would seem that his son took his father's advice to heart for he never missed an opportunity to whack us with his boot-slapping stick. There didn't have to be a reason; you were beaten as a deterrent not as a punishment. We were beaten because he liked the power or rather the chance to abuse his power because he could. It was as casually administered as taking a biscuit from a jar.

At the school itself the policy of child beating was that it be carried out by one brother but occasionally there were two brothers present. This was when a major beating was being carried out. I can only presume this was because there needed to be a witness, hardly a hostile one, if the effects of the beating were so severe as to warrant medical or outside intervention.

The beatings inflicted on me continued and I could expect them to occur twice each week. My behavior, which was invariably good, had no bearing on the matter. All I could think of was, fuck those bastards. I will do whatever I can to fuck them up behind their backs.

The days were rolling by from one to the other and the harsh routine of each day's work was broken only be the Friday meal when you received on your plate what was supposed to be fish. Other than that there was just the thought that each small ritual milestone heralded another seven days of backbreaking soul-destroying work. The dairy herd needed constant attention and being the bad boys we were not allowed the luxury of a break; thus the work was to be our lives as long as we were at Letterfrack.

We learned that pissing on our hands brought some relief when they became blistered. Yes, even milking cattle teats causes blisters when it is done twice a day seven days a week. Children's hands aren't really strong enough for that kind of work in which there is never a period for recovery.

As time went by and the weather seemed to improve in harmony with the days growing longer there came the day when I was called up to see the head brother. Shite, I thought. What have I done now? I had learned that it wasn't necessary for me to do anything at all to merit a beating or a command that I appear before the brother's head.

Would I be sent to Dangein Industrial School? That place had an appalling reputation and it was said to be far worse than was Letterfrack. As I found later on in life, there was no school worse than Letterfrack; not even Dangein.

As I stood outside the brother's door I was petrified at the thought of what might await me once called in. The fifteen minutes I did waited seemed to last an eternity. These brothers were entirely devoid of compassion or conscience. They would be well aware of the trepidation on youngsters' faces as they awaited their summons. The opportunity for inflicting suffering offered the prospect of pushing the boundaries. I had only once been into his office and I had horrific recall of the beating he had inflicted on me. To them a beating was an outlet, a self-indulgence to break the monotony of their own lives.

Once I was called I entered to find him sat behind his desk whilst I stood respectfully before it with my hands behind my back. From the comfort of his large leather seat he peered over his glasses at me.

"You seem to be something of an abnormality." he says. That makes two of us I thought to myself.

"You're fourteen are you not?"

I nodded my head; my birthday had just passed; not that they would notice.

He went on: "You are a loner and I have thought up a job for you that will leave you to your own devices. You will have my trust in you to do and say only what you are told. You will work with the farmer who will train you in sheep husbandry. Do you understand?"

I was unsure of what he wanted from me but liked the idea of working on my own devises. Nodding my head I said in a low voice. "Yes."

He looked at me with what he thought must be a benign manner: "You will of course have long days and you will work solely in the confines of this school's boundaries, to which you must adhere to at all cost. If you have any problems, or if at anytime you feel the urge to run away, then you must come and see me. We shall iron out any problems that you may have. Do you understand?"

Again I nodded and replied in the affirmative. He looked thoughtfully for a long minute as though he himself was wondering if there might be something further to add: "You mustn't let me down, boy."

I was in a state of bewilderment as I left his office and couldn't figure out why I had been transferred to such a preferential job that carried with it the opportunity for escape but trust to counter it. Little did I then realise that the work was not preferential. I had at least done what I hoped was my last milking session and as I snuggled down into my bed I could only wonder what the next day might bring.

I got a bit of a lie-in as usually I was up and on my way long before Brother Chinney arrived to clap his hands and wake everyone and get them on their feet beside their beds. Then, after the usual morning routine and with my lunch tucked under my arm I made my way to the farmyard. The rest of the boys were on a short break and wondering what I was doing arriving a little late with my lunch pack.

The farmer was there of course as was his son. I hoped that I would not be working on my own with him. I could never trust him. My mind was eased; he was put in charge of the others who would be doing the milking.

The farmer was a man probably in his early fifties; roughly dressed as farmers are; a rotund almost caricature of a figure with a huge gut and spindly legs. Constantly smoking his pipe it was as much a part of him as was one of his limbs.

There were two dogs with him; both collies one of which was old and white. It was called Driver whilst its companion was black with white patches. I guessed it to be about 12 months old so like me it was still growing and learning. For some reason this dog was called Swim.

Setting off with the dogs ambling beside us those two occasionally ran ahead or paused to take in their surroundings. I had guessed right. Swim like me was in training to be a shepherd. Striking out across the pastures and up the mountain's side we could see Letterfrack Industrial School set out in the valley just as though it was a model in an architect's office.

As we made our way to the pastures where the sheep were grazing my work was explained to me. My job was to keep the sheep within the boundaries of the lines. These were clearly defined by the fences but these were not always in evidence on our territory. There had been some cost cutting and the fences had not been properly maintained if they had been placed in position in the first place. This meant the sheep could wander at will and cover miles in a day's grazing. My job was to track the wanderers down and bring them back. Given the size of the territory this was an almost impossible undertaking. My day would start at 8.00am and finish at either the fall of darkness or teatime, whichever came first.

Without a watch I wouldn't know when it was near tea time I told him. His reply was that I should keep my ears open for the noise from the playground as this would indicate the time I could leave Otherwise I would soon get used to keeping the time in my head. During the first two days he would stay with me so I could get used to herding the sheep and instructing the dogs.

By now with some apprehension I was looking forward to a solitary lifestyle when I would have the day all to myself.

It was a steep learning curve and I was confused as trying to get to grips with instructing the dogs with different whistle sounds and tones didn't come easily. For some reason the dogs didn't respond to me as they did the farmer. This meant I had to do their job for them; running around and bringing in the stragglers, keeping the rest together and this was far from easy. I must have made a real sight; a half-starved skinny kid dressed in shorts and Wellington boots, stick in hand running around in circles screaming at dumb sheep that peered at me with blank disinterest; it must be said with very little initial success.

I soon learned to say things like 'Driver away out', 'Come in now'. It was all gibberish to me and my Dublin accent was so far removed from the farmer's that I must have seemed to the dogs to be speaking in a foreign language. I persevered and after a few days I was managing to exert some kind of control over the sheepdogs. The sheep were the biggest problem; they did have minds of their own and exercised their independence of thought with enthusiasm. I was soon to learn that this is the way of the beasts; the dumb looks are deceptive and they can be as clever as we are and I had to live with it.

By the following Monday I was judged to be proficient and at last I was on my own up there in the hills; just me, the two dogs and of course the sheep. Each morning proud as could be I would set off with the dogs with a spring in my step. When out on the mountain the farmer was happy enough to let me get on with it and just occasionally he would turn up seemingly from nowhere. This didn't cause me a problem. I was happy enough being a shepherd boy.

Each day was different so it was far from being a boring occupation. The sheep saw to it that I was kept busy and at the end of the day it could be hard work grouping them together before driving them back to their pens.

I have no idea how many miles I traipsed each day but there must have been many of them.

One day when heading in a westward direction I could see in the far distance what appeared to be a group of people but it could as easily have been cattle; they were that far away. I could see they weren't sheep. With the dogs in tow I allowed my curiosity to pull me in the direction of the strange sight and drawing closer could see it was a small group of men.

As the distance between us became less they paused in their tracks and looking at me seemed to wait until I closed with them. I had no idea who they were and they looked so out of place up there in the hills. I was thinking, shite. Have I messed up? Are they something to do with the brothers because if they are I am in deep shit because I am now off my territory and without an excuse?

They were in fact land surveyors, two of them being from Dublin.

As I approached it was evident that they were both curious and friendly and as soon as we drew close enough to speak one of them greeted me and asked what a lad like me was doing out there in the wilderness and not dressed properly for the weather conditions. The dogs clustered around my ankles so I felt a little in control of the situation.

"I am a shepherd," I told them. "I am looking for some strays. You wouldn't happen to have seen them?"

One of them chuckled and asked if I was from the school, nodding his head in the direction of Letterfrack as he did so. I told them I was from the school but that I was also a shepherd. I was proud of the position and the trust.

"Good lad. You're from Dublin?" As he spoke he indicated his companion standing nearest to him. "So is he; we both are and so you are too judging from your accent."

He went on to explain that they were making land surveys and then asked if there was anything they might do for me. I cheekily asked them if they had any fags. The way they then looked at each other I thought they were going to report me to the brothers but to my amazement and delight they each took a pack of cigarettes from their pockets. As casual as ever they took several cigarettes from each and handed me a bundle of them. They also handed me a pack of matches.

"Keep them dry and safe, lad. And you had better be getting back otherwise they will be looking for you."

Grinning and with the first of the cigarettes between my lips I waved them goodbye and turned on my heel. The small event in a routine day was a memory to be cherished but I didn't push my luck. I saw them working in the distance on several further occasions but never again approached them.

I knew the brothers didn't want us talking to outsiders. I valued my job and had no interest in putting it at risk.

I often thought that maybe the reason the head brother had given me the job was based on shrewdness. From where I worked I could see far into the distance and the landscape might easily have been the earth's edge. It was a constant reminder of the remoteness of the area and the impossibility of traversing it unseen. The distance was its own a prison wall and as such its own deterrent. Perhaps he had another reason. Was there somewhere in his dark soul a respect for my stoicism? I shall never know but I was grateful for the freedom the job brought with it.

Being away from the school each day meant I had no idea what was going on down there. I relied on the church services for opportunity to find out what if anything was happening. There was nothing for me to concern myself with. Nothing had changed; there were the usual beatings and abuses being carried out including sexual molestation.

There were boys who for reasons of survival were happy to act as concubines and others more reluctant.

We looked on them as a form of beating and if such behavior could be avoided then we did so; there wasn't any views held on the matter. They were in fact similar for the brothers obviously took pleasure in inflicting pain and humiliation; sexual or otherwise.

Nothing was going to change every child's nightmare and I couldn't have been happier being where I was up in the hills and well away from it. I weathered the harsh conditions well. It occasionally rained at which times I could hardly see from one hill to another but then the sheep were less likely to wander so there was compensation of sorts. The winds blew cold at the beginning and end of each day but I learned to minimize the chill. Either that or

I simply acclimatized to it. There was nothing with which I could make comparisons.

It was during one of the summer mornings and it appeared there was hardly more than me and the wildlife present when my ear caught a whimpering sound. I was heading for the bogs at the time and increased my step so better to see where the sounds of distress were coming from. It wasn't long before I came across a small dog trapped in a barbed wire fence. The barbs had entangled in its hair and trying to extricate itself it had only made matters worse and in places its flesh was torn. I thought I recognized it as the doctor's small terrier and to me it looked like it was in a bad way.

Gently and cautiously so as to not hurt it further I untangled him from the wire but then was caught in a further predicament. It was late in the day. If I were to carry the injured animal back to the farm then it would leave me too little time to return, gather the sheep together and get them to their pens.

I had little choice but to leave the little feller where I had found him; get on with my tasks and take him with us when we descended the hilltop pastures. I went about my business and when it was time to return and pick him up there was no sign of the injured animal. This left me with another predicament. What do I do now? It seemed that I could be in trouble for abandoning the distressed creature.

When I and my little herd poured once again through the farm gates I told the farmer of the drama. I explained also the predicament I was in had I abandoned the sheep to bring the dog to him. He said he would take care of the problem and he would tell the doctor. It occurred to me that I should have carried the mite with me for the day; he wasn't that heavy. Hindsight being a wonderful thing it seemed to me that the dog might have added to its problems by getting lost and even getting into further trouble. Was it now lost for good due to my carelessness?

Before heading off the next morning I was called to the head brother's office. It was the first time I had been there since I was given the shepherd's job. Again I blasphemed and bit my bottom lip as I contemplated my fate. The worst hellhole on earth was to go through the door of a brother's home office; especially the head of the brothers. I wondered if word had got back to him that I had been seen in the company of the surveying team.

Little did I know that the farmer had watched my every move that day? He had been following my settling in process from a distance by using his binoculars. It had been fortunate that my meeting them had happened only on the one occasion; I hate to imagine the consequences had he told the brothers.

On this occasion I need not have worried too much. He wanted to see me about the matter of the dog: "Did you have anything to do with the disappearance of the dog," he enquired of me.

I told him I hadn't and explained how I had come across the dog, found it trapped and badly hurt. On freeing it I didn't think it was capable of moving and planned to bring it down from the hills with me when I returned with the sheep a little later.

Again he appeared thoughtful and then finally said that it was okay, he was going to give me the benefit of the doubt and I should now go off and get on with my work.

On reaching the farm who should I see there but the doctor holding her dog in her arms? The mutt had arrived home during the night and she had since heard the story of my kindness both in freeing her dog and of my intentions.

Handing me a big bag of sweets she thanked me for my kindness and for rescuing her dog from the barbed wire trap. The sweets and thanks were well received but again it was a reminder that you ran the risk of being wronged when you were motivated only by good.

Chapter 14

This time when the summer holidays arrived I was under no illusions about whether I would be staying or going home. In a way it helped as there were no expectations to be dashed. I had already made my mind up to make the most of the swimming excursions.

All went much as expected; a carbon copy of earlier holidays and excursions. We all got much out of the visits to the cove where we dived, jumped and otherwise swam to our heart's content. There were country walks to be enjoyed but above all else there were the sheep to be looked after. I was happy enough in my own little world and it was a long time since I had been beaten the shit out of by a brother who just felt like doing so.

Out of sight was out of mind. The scars had healed but not the ones left on the heart and mind. Our souls remember the small acts of love and charity; regretfully the soul also remembers the acts of malevolent cruelty. Up there in the hills the time was passing more quickly; perhaps because up there I was a free spirit and a free spirit doesn't recognize time with all of its restrictions and controls. I was glad I didn't have a watch. The farmer had been right; the clock in my head kept perfect time.

Driver and Swim had learned to recognize my accent and we had become a team of three equals. They were a great help to me when we were rounding up the sheep. They responded well, especially to my frequent head pats and stroking.

Swim was the most boisterous and free-spirited and could be a nuisance. He knew what it was to get a mouthful but taking all into consideration life was as good as it was ever going to get at Letterfrack. Yes, there were no more beatings and my body clock was ticking away; I was constantly reminding myself that my sentence was coming to an end.

Could any child ever have suffered so much for an unsociable prank; was ever a can of soft drinks valued so much; a few coins sprinkled on a social cub's floors?

The job meant I could not have taken part in the Christmas play that year but it was a small price to pay for my freedoms. Another advantage was I actually got the opportunity to watch the play. This year I wouldn't be sobbing against the wall with my back to it.

The days had grown shorter as summer slipped into autumn and by the time nightfall was drawing closer to dinner time the weather had turned. There were the occasional days that were comfortable enough but up there in the exposed hillsides I was beginning to feel the wrath of the Atlantic storms. When the wind turned and came from the north or east I felt the chill despite the shelter. If it rained it came down in stair rods and of course there was only nature's shelter to be had. A tree's hollow, a stone wall behind which I could cower. Then more than ever I thought about it being my last winter here

Down there in the industrial school there was no escape from the constant fear of a brother's unaccountable wrath.

Such attacks were quite unpredictable. If they were in any way predictable it was when they were least expected or undeserved. I sometimes wonder if that was part of the strategy of terror; the unexpectedness and their being random. A child would hear his voice being called and the terror would still his heart. He knew he was in for a beating. Why would there be a need for a reason? The purpose was the holistic installation of terror and enforced discipline. It was a constant reminder of the brothers' all-powerfulness. There was purpose behind the arbitrary nature of it.

The only protection was to adopt a low profile and at all times maintain total servility. It was no guarantee you wouldn't be selected for casual cruelties; it merely reduced the chances.

It was sadly a time when it was heartbreaking but a relief when someone's name other than your own was called. We all knew what the unfortunate child was going to be subjected to; we had each felt the blows; heard the uttered oaths as the blows fell. Ours had to be a yes sir, no sir; three bags full, sir option for a hoped for pain-free existence.

Here the natural laws of right and wrong, justice and injustice had been suspended. The brothers were always right whilst we were always wrong. It was why we had been sent there; this included the orphans who had never done wrong to anyone. They lost their mothers and fathers; they lost their freedom, their dignity, and they lost their childhood too.

Was ever a title ever so sadly misplaced for this was the last place on earth where one might expect brotherly love?

The infliction of calculated and random terror had the desired effect. No one had absconded since my futile attempt followed by the savage beatings and the months on non-stop running around the yard. This followed by the kick in the guts for no other reason than to inflict torment. The deterrent worked well; the Garda could sleep easily in their beds at night. Heaven forbid they might be called upon to track down a distressed child.

I got through that winter and with Christmas and the New Year out of the way the lambing season got into full swing. I could never work out why it started so early because the newborn creatures often arrived when the temperatures were below freezing and the sleet and snow was still piling up against the sheltering walls. Whatever, it was nature in the raw and most of them did survive. It was a wonderful experience to be a part of for I found it easy to empathize with each of the mothers. Their newborn would stagger to their uncertain feet whilst still shaking off the afterbirth and before you knew it they would be celebrating life itself.

What on earth possessed them other than the pure joy as they frolicked among themselves? It seemed as though they had small bedsprings in their feet. But, they are mountain creatures and their instincts were inbred. Did they the lambs give a genesis to the cry of maaaa, maaaaa?

Some of the mother sheep were not much better than were humans; most were happy to stay close and provide suckling and refuge. Others were not so maternal and when the kids were abandoned then it was down to us to bottle feed them. Those mothers were no better than their human counterparts who leave their babies outside churches or placed in baskets at hospital main entrances. Has the human race justification in thinking of itself as superior to the animal kingdom when the opposite seems so often to be the case?

To me the birth event was a beautiful and an amazing sight to see and I would do all in my power to save any unfortunate lamb I found abandoned. Some of these creatures didn't last long; abandoned or just too weak to withstand the weather. In such cases I had to bring the small bodies down with me but I always cradled them respectfully. To me they were even more precious than those that lived for they had suffered the trauma of birth but not the joys of life itself.

Up in those sometimes forbidding hills set behind the school some unknown person from way back had carved out a small cave and fortified its entrance with boulders, For me it was the perfect retreat from the weather, especially when I could disappear into it and enjoy my lunch. I reveled in the security of its walls and my being out of sight. It was very much as if I had disappeared temporarily from all of the earth's troubles.

It was my domain and I would spend many a pleasing half hour in there just dreaming of what used to be. One recurring theme was the day I went with my ma to the docks to see my da.

I suppose at the time I would have been about five-years old and we then lived in Railway Terrace. Da was a seaman during our time there and he would be away for long periods of time; for as long as six months. The day arrived when my ma got a telegram to say he would be home on such and such a day. Naturally ma was over the moon at hearing the news.

To my vivid recollection she was up before dawn; washed and dressed in best clothes normally used only on a Sunday. I couldn't shut her up as she got me dressed and prepared our breakfast. I don't think I had ever seen her chatter so much. As she was keeping me off school for the occasion I was almost as excited, certainly expectant at seeing my da again. As soon as our breakfasts were down us we set off. I knew the route well. Into Macken Street then cross over Pearce Street heading in the direction of the River Liffey which separates the city. In no time at all we would pass the gasometer and be at the quays.

As soon as we got there we boarded the small ferry boat that took us across to the far side. It was all a great adventure for me; being helped on and off the boat by the ferryman. The workers who mostly used it were well ahead of us and so we had the boat to ourselves. Off we trotted hand in hand past the goods yard and along the dock walls. It was a long walk but even so I took everything in; the Alexandra dock gates and the wharfs where the bigger ships lay moored.

This is where the disappointment set in for there was no ship bearing the name of my da's ship. We waited patiently, went to a café then returned to wait a little longer. We must have looked a sight and at some point when dark was closing in we were approached by a dock worker. He chatted to my mum for a little while and we learned that according to their roster da's ship wouldn't be docking until next week. Ma just said she was wondering why we were the only ones there as we set off to return home.

This was not as pleasant as our walk to the docks. Ma was ranting and raving about my da never getting anything right and anyway, he would always go to his mother's house first before showing any interest in his wife and children. This meant da had to duck under our window ledge as his mother's house was three doors further down our terrace. The recollections of that particular failed excursion somehow stayed with me for the rest of my life and hunched up in my hillside cave with my knees tucked under my chin I thought about every step of that futile journey.

Da did come home the following week. His ship had been to the United States and he had brought lots of presents for us. I remember jackets that could be worn inside out; quite a novelty at the time. Ma got a wonderful music box and yes, he did go to his mother's first.

In fairness to him the fault could be traced back to a clerk at the shipping agent's offices who had sent the telegram. Da had no part in it being sent. We were all victims as da had no one to meet him when he did arrive and had wondered why.

Such were my reminiscences that marked the passage of time in the hills overlooking Letterfrack. Easter was now drawing near; the days were longer and the winds were less biting cold. Each morning there continued to be the ritual of going to mass; then repeat it during the evening; mass, Stations of the Cross and the Rosary; there was no escaping the rites. It was all to ensure we didn't become stray lambs and that we remained true to the one god, but no one had asked our permission first. No one had asked if we wanted to believe in this god; it was taken as gospel that we would follow the religious path chosen for us.

By this time I think I can describe myself as a professional shepherd; certainly as good as shepherds go.

I can handle the dogs like an expert and I bet I could win competitions with the both of them. We worked so well together despite the fact that Swim can still be a juvenile delinquent when it suits him. I have never been so contented in my life; I loved my job and the openness of the countrywide; it too seems to be a free spirit when I am as one with it. It is also a constant reminder of the folly of trying to escape. As far as the eye can see there is just the barren bog and the glowering mountains blocking every escape route? Only now did I realise the futility of my earlier escapades.

Apart from the one time when I met the group of surveyors I never encountered another living soul. The loneliness up there was in sharp contrast to the bustle on the Easter Sunday. It is of course a big day and the locals are all togged out in their best outfits and being nice and polite to each other. One cannot deny how beautiful the women look in their fine dresses. The weather is complementary for it is a warm sunny day. This in itself was unusual because my recollections of Easter Sundays are their being damp and miserable.

The big day came and went as one might expect and during the evening we all trooped in to watch a film. It was about a young girl taking communion; quite a sad and thoughtful film for us to see before retiring to our beds. It is also the time when from the Tuesday the only great event to look forward to are the summer holidays. My behavior has been exemplary this year and I wonder if my past sins have been forgotten and if not perhaps they have been forgiven. If they can sin and be let off the hook with a visit to the confessionary and an act of contrition then why cannot I too? Will I be allowed to go home for the summer holiday this year?

Naturally I am on my best behavior when the brothers are around and I have really set my heart on going home.

But apart from the daily rituals everything else seems to be very much the caprice of the moment. There is never a hint at who might and might not be going; the anticipation is nerve wracking.

From what I was to later gather there is an organised procedure for doing things the brothers' way. From the moment you arrive the brothers between them discuss which of them will be responsible for you. That you would be induced one way or another to fall into the correct mindset and it would even be decided if there might be opportunity for sex with a newcomer. Whatever, the regime certainly included a physical aspect and an unremitting presumption that your servility might be counted upon. One way or another it was going to happen; it was their goal. If you were to rebel then they would simply hone their skills at persuasion by whatever means they thought necessary. There was an unspoken law that implied full compliance; brothers' and children alike.

Only as the time for your release approached would the abuse lessen for by then they had either achieved their objective or failed. Besides, they did not want fresh memories. The vaguer about times a victim was then the better it suited them. They didn't like short memories. They counted on your being so relieved at being freed the abuse that had marked your term would be soon forgotten, eclipsed completely by the experience of being independent. They were anyway guaranteed a constant supply of victims. It stopped them getting bored and new arrivals were always relished.

My daily routine as a shepherd continued and before long June was just a week or so away and we were all holding our breath as to who might and might not be going home; apart from the orphans of course. I often wondered what was in their minds at times like this. Or do I wish to think such thoughts? Perhaps it is best not to.

Chapter 15

The newcomers had no chance of being selected and there being so many for there had been a steady stream of arrivals. This had narrowed the choices down to us older internees. From the intake it seemed our country had a big problem with delinquent children. A better solution might have been for the shadowy string-pullers to get around the table and figure out why this was happening; why unsociable behavior was not a big in other European countries. Was it because their societies cared better for their children and that concern was returned by a sense of juvenile responsibility rather than rebelliousness at the afflictions of a dysfunctional society? Are the harshly run prisons in the remote countryside the answer to society's failings? If so where are the Letterfrack's for the politicians and their lickspittle cronies? The truth of the matter is they simply did not care; the requisite solution was out of sight, out of mind.

There we were, all scrumming about in the school yard awaiting the roll call when the word goes round that the head brother has appeared and the names are about to be announced.

We all line up in our usual formation and eagerly await the news. Joy upon joy! I discover that my name is called as having been favored with a home visit. I can hardly contain my excitement and can't wait to write to ma and share my good news. I have just four weeks to kill and it certainly adds pleasure to my job as a shepherd. There is a spring in my step that would delight any lamb, jauntiness in my striding about with the dogs and my eyes must have been shining brightly. All I need worry about is will any mishap mess things up.

It was a Friday afternoon and not long to go before the day the bus would arrive. I was instructed to be at the head brother's office at seven-thirty the following morning. I am mortified at the news.

What on earth could I have done wrong to justify such a visit, especially on a Saturday morning? This was unheard of except in the most compelling cases. Needless to say I hardly slept that very long night.

I am awake long before Brother Chinney begins his clapping and one of the first to wash. It is then that I tell Chinney I am to report to the head brother's office. He tells me he is aware of the fact and tells me to run off so I am not late. There was little for me to worry about and no standing outside his office door. The head brother is already outside and a warm smile of welcome is on his face. "Don't look so terrified, boy. You and I are off to Galway and you are to accompany me."

I learn that there is a dog show being held in the city. Perhaps my relationship with my own dogs has marked me out as the most appropriate companion. He is taking the two Red Setters with us. They are already in the back of the car when he invites me to hop in. There was a silence for awhile and we were well on the road to Galway before he broke it.

"You will be going home on holidays soon," he said quietly: "No doubt you will be taking home good memories of how well you have been treated here and of how good we have all been to you since your last escape. How good I have been to you," he said as though talking to himself: "Yes, how good I have been to you and what a good job I acquired for you."

"Yes, sir," I conceded in almost a whisper whilst inside my stomach was churning and I was thinking to myself: Fuck you, you shite; you have never been good to me. But this was no time for telling the truth so I held my tongue. This was the approach of my holiday and the year of my release. Nothing must jeopardize either.

We continued to travel on in silence and my thoughts were taken up by the wonderful views as the car swept along the country lanes on this lovely weekend morning.

As we swept through one village after another I briefly recalled my escape. Having already travelled so far in the car and with Galway yet to be reached the senselessness of my escape became even more sharply into focus.

There were people out and about, shopping, and gossiping, going about their daily business; all of which had passed me by when two years earlier we had passed through the same villages by bus.

We must have been getting closer to Galway for the head brother once again broke his silence. He reminded me that we were going to a dog show and whilst it was clear that I was not a happy lad, though I should be, I must cheer up and be on my best behavior.

"Don't worry, brother," I said. "I won't be letting you down."

Shortly afterwards we drove through some large and ornate open gates and then followed a drive leading up to a large stately home. In fact it was a religious convent and outside were parked a multitude of cars, many lined up on the grass against a backdrop of tents and tables.

Parking the car we got the two dogs out, both of which were put on leads before setting out in the direction of the biggest of the tents. This was where we were to register the dogs. The head brother seemed to know a lot of the people attending and there was much handshaking and conviviality. I might just as well have been invisible as they knew any kid in the company of the brother was an outcast and to be treated as such. The only thing that struck me was that I had no recollection of any other kid accompanying the brother to a dog show.

I wasn't too worried about what people thought about me and was content enough to take in my surroundings as I walked along in the company of the brother. The hours passed with dogs doing all kinds of tricks, following commands and being admired or criticized.

At one stage we went into another tent for tea and sandwiches. These had a funny green thing in them that didn't appeal to me at all. I tried to get around the problem by swallowing it rather than chewing whatever it was. As a consequence I very nearly choked myself.

The brother's Red Setters won two ribbons and he was delighted with this. This was followed by much handshaking and farewells as we loaded the dogs back aboard the car and set off on our return journey to the school.

Before reaching Letterfrack he half turned towards me and said he probably wouldn't have another opportunity to speak to me before I went on holiday. He then impressed upon me the importance of keeping in mind that I was been well looked after. That I must have a good holiday and he promised me that he would keep me in mind for future dog shows. He added that my job as a shepherd was assured if I was well behaved and despite my past bad behavior I was appreciative of the brother's efforts to reform me.

I murmured that I would be happy and under the circumstances I had no trouble with lying to him. Nothing would ever heal the scars of the treatment I had received at the hands of him and his fellow brothers. They were too deep, constantly painful and always humiliating. I was now fifteen and a half years old and not particularly intelligent in an academic way. Nevertheless I did know the difference between right and wrong.

I knew too that ultimately he was responsible for everything that went on at the school and that he more than anyone else should be held to account but that does not seem to happen in Ireland no one is responsible. Today's event had nothing at all to do with my wellbeing but on account of his.

I can still picture the looks I was getting from the other boys after we returned. It seemed to them that I had been offering a little more to the head brother than I wished them to know. Even the younger kids were looking at me in a strange sort of way, which I felt very uncomfortable with.

The few remaining weeks passed without incident and on the night preceding the arrival of the bus the anticipation could be felt if not heard in the tossing of bedclothes and the whispers that went from bed to bed. I was awake long before the fucking clapping. Little did I know that I was never again to hear it save in my memory: It was July and 1967 the year.

Like sheep trying to get through a gap in a country wall we pushed and shoved our way up the steps of the bus and as we did so we were slapped about our heads to remind us we must board in an orderly fashion. No singing was allowed and as I looked around the other boys I realised that many of them were about my age and unlikely to be here at Letterfrack for very much longer.

On our arrival at the railway station we seemed less subdued than on the earlier occasion but the brothers didn't seem to mind our unruliness. This seemed so out of character. We all crowded on to the platform and despite our high spirits not one of the brothers raised his voice. It was then I noticed a group of servicemen with their kitbags over their shoulders. It occurred to me the brothers might have been aware of some ex-pupils among them who might confront them if they saw the brothers being abusive towards us.

Boarding the train off we went to Dublin and on this joyful occasion again singing We're off to Dublin in the Green over and over again. There was an almost Christmas jollity about it all with everyone looking at us and smiling. Were we once again rejoining the human race; were we no longer society's debris?

I had enough other things to worry about, such as what or who awaited me on my arrival in Dublin. I did know I had a new baby brother and the family had moved out of North Great Georges Street but to where I had no idea at all.

On our arrival at Kings Bridge Station I looked but couldn't see my ma anywhere in the milling crowd. I was quite worried; it was inconceivable she wouldn't be here to greet me. It was then I heard a call coming from my right: "Is that you, Mickey?"

Looking around I saw standing there my uncle. He was in fact my older brother but that was a revelation yet to come. "Over here," he shouted: "Over here!"

Going over to him I greeted him and asked where ma was. He told me she couldn't make it today; it was better that he meet me and he reminded me she and my family had moved home. "Look," he said holding out a bag: "I bought you some sweets."

The pair of us set out following the usual route through the Quays but this time we were heading towards O' Connell Street. Curious, I asked him where we had moved to. All he would say was: "You'll see."

Pausing he smiled and then said: "It is a brand new house. It is in the countryside and big enough to be a ranch. "Come on; we will cross Eden Bridge and catch a bus. It will only take us half an hour."

As we climbed aboard the bus he asked me if I had ever heard of the Beatles. He told me he was in a band and regularly played at church halls. I explained I had been living in what can best be described as a wilderness and that we never ever heard a radio, watched television or even saw a newspaper. We had been completely isolated from the outside world.

When we finally alighted I could only describe our surroundings as being a building site through which we had quite a walk ahead of us before reaching our new home. As soon as we arrived I spotted ma waiting for us and beside her a new pram with my new brother in it. Otherwise the house was empty. Da was out at work and I was informed there were prospects of our emigrating to Australia. She let it be known that the idea didn't appeal to her at all.

With a lot of 'hold him tightly' advice I was allowed to hold my little mite of a brother and then shown the bedroom

I was to share with my younger brother. The room itself was quite long with two beds, one at each end. "Look," ma said: "Isn't it wonderful?"

Not entirely unexpectedly ma had made a delicious coddle for me and I wolfed it down as my 'uncle' left us to ourselves. As he cheerily went on his way he called that he would be picking me up at the weekend to take me to see his band performing.

In the living room a television and a fireplace. There was a front and back garden but the downside was there were neither shops nor a pub nearby. They had to catch a bus into town when there was shopping to be done and da could be counted upon to be on the last bus after the pub had closed. He had changed his watering hole and was now drinking on Eden Quay; there he could be found all of any weekend.

During the working week he would leave on the first bus which was called the Dockers bus. He worked near the docks on East Wall doing long distance truck driving which took him all over Ireland.

Of course I knew nobody where we were now living but was quite happy to watch the television during the evenings and to take long walks with my younger brother in the afternoons.

The school holidays were on and most of our conversation was taken up with me impressing upon him the need for him to get a proper education and to never ever get into the wrong company or into trouble of any kind. I remarked that from bitter experience so-called mates had no problem at all leading you into the shite but were happy enough to leave you there if you got stuck in it. I told him he must always put what was best for him first and if ever in any doubt then he must call on me.

I wanted to be the big brother I never had. The two elder brothers I did have thought it my duty to put their interests before my own.

The following week, as previously arranged, my 'uncle' arrived and what followed was a two bus ride that took us to my Nan's house in Ringsend. She was overjoyed at seeing me, remarking all the time how I had changed and pressing ten shillings into my hand fluttered about me like a mother hen.

Not surprisingly I had little or no idea of the value of money; I wasn't aware of its essential nature for throughout my life I had presumed to be fed and bed. It had rarely occurred to me I would need to earn and be independent. I was now approaching my sixteenth birthday and was soon to find out what the real world was all about. My childhood had gone; it had passed me by and I was now near adulthood.

After a chips and eggs supper we pair set off for the night's gig; it was to be in a church hall in the Crumlin district. There were to be three bands that night and my uncle's was to play second with the major band The Bye Laws playing last. The hall was packed with kids, boys and girls and it was a memorable night that was to leave a lasting impression on me.

From there on I was to find great solace and enjoyment in music.

I never learned to play an instrument but I was an avid purchaser of records and much of my later in life was spent travelling to major gigs.

It was necessary for me to stay at my Nan's that night as there was no public transport but on the Sunday morning we set off on our way back to the new house. I say 'we' but my uncle left me at the bus stop at Eden Quay. My mother must have got tired of hearing about my enthusiasm for the previous night's gig and how everyone was dancing around and whooping things along. It had been a fabulous new experience.

I think it was then I was to make my mind up that I was not going to go back to Letterfrack. I was going to abscond but this time home was to be where the running started. So when it got closer to the day I was to return to Letterfrack I told my ma I had decided I was not going back to the industrial school in Connemara. I would never tell her how bad it was but I was adamant I was not going back there.

On hearing of my decision da went ballistic but in the end he said it's on your shoulders, lad. If they catch you it will probably mean more time and that will be down to you. He asked me where I intended to live and how I expected to keep myself. Obviously you cannot stay here he reminded me.

I told him I would find somewhere to live and for him not to concern himself. After some discussion with ma it was decided I would have to get a job and lie low until I was sixteen. It was da's beliefs that after that age the brothers could do fuck all to me. I would from Saturday on be on the run for three months. Knowing well the likely consequences of my being returned there was no question about the importance of staying out of their reach.

Saturday, my day of no return arrived and on the Monday I got a job in a factory filling shampoo bottles.

It was a long walk to and from work but I was delighted to have the job and my freedom; it was a small price to pay for becoming human. I had been of less value than a farm animal for long enough.

It took about a week for the brothers to turn up. It was on a Monday evening and for once my da was at home having decided to turn the garden over. He was out in front with the shovel in his hands when the car pulled up outside.

Two of the brothers clambered out; one was Chinney and the other a big brute of a man I didn't recognize. I was peeking out through the curtains and could see another brother and two kids in the car's rear seat.

Downstairs I could hear da remonstrating with them. "He is not here, you fuckers. Now clear off before I have at you with this shovel."

With that Chinney tried to come through the front gate but my da grabbed him and dragging him into the garden and holding him by his throat started to strangle him. It was then that the bigger of the two brothers came to Chinney's rescue and the other brother leapt from the car to join in the brawl. It was Brother Tea, the bastard.

As soon as he had leaped from the car, leaving the vehicle's door open, the two kids inside leaped free and ran off up the road. Da hurled Chinney to the ground and lifting the shovel high above his head as though tempted to bring it down on the head of the hapless brother. As he did so he shouted at the two other brothers: "Get out of my fucking garden now, you scum. Out now or suffer the consequences." With that they left and climbed back into their car. By this time the two youngsters were well out of sight.

I often wonder what the outcome would have been if my da realised just how badly I had been treated; not just me but the others boys too, especially by those pure-bred evil bastards, Brother Chinney and Brother Tea.

That was the last I was to ever see of them. The Garda never came looking for me and so in the end I had successfully escaped. Scarred? Yes, I avoided the last few months there but more than forty years were to pass before I could come to terms with those awful events and for posterity if nothing else to record them.

I kept my job until I reached sixteen years of age.

Despite da's earlier concerns for me, so valiantly expressed during the confrontation with the brothers, we never quite saw eye to eye on a number of issues. There was much more that separated us than bound us together. He loved the drink; a weakness I despised for it can bring so much misery with over indulgence.

I was earning enough to get my own small flat and after some searching found the perfect one on the south Circular Road at just three pounds a week. I was earning three pounds ten shillings per week but I was a loner; the shepherd still and was able to survive on this until things were to change.

In my thoughts was the heartfelt wish to forget Letterfrack; to consider it a void in my life; to make a leap of faith across a chasm that covered a near four year span of a child's life. It was never my intention to even discuss it; for me it never happened. It was a nightmare and nightmares are best forgotten.

I wanted to let go of Letterfrack and move on but it would never take its brother's boot off my neck.

Whatever was to confront me later in life the malevolent long-reaching grasp of that awful boys' penitentiary would reach out, tap me on my shoulder and remind me I would always be shackled, a prisoner of my past. Whenever I tried to move on; get a job, move abroad it would hover like an avenging dark angel of misery. I was still being punished whilst the guilty were left free to reach deeper and ever deeper into depravity.

Nothing would be held against our abusers because they were the certified State's abusers. It they were to be condemned then so would the State. They knew, the Garda, the officials, the civil servants; those in public life knew what was going on in the so-called industrial schools. They drew the curtains across and left their consciences on the other side.

Governments come and go but the system is always there; it was never in the interests of The Dail [parliament's] new faces to lift the lid on the iniquities that might be laid at the doors of the predecessors or their system for they were of the same ilk. In Ireland as elsewhere there is a rotating dictatorship between two parties that ostensibly oppose each other but it is public sparring to keep alive the myth of democracy. In reality they all piss in the same pot after drinking from the same cup. There is but one religious entity and for them there was just denial and of course the whispered words, perhaps, in the confessional box. The only ones in the triangle of death left to speak are the victims for they alone have nothing to hide. ©